Elite • 180

US Coast Guard
in World War II

ALEJANDRO DE QUESADA   ILLUSTRATED BY STEPHEN WALSH

Consultant editor Martin Windrow

First published in Great Britain in 2010 by Osprey Publishing,
Midland House, West Way, Botley, Oxford OX2 0PH, UK
44-02 23rd St, Suite 219, Long Island City, NY 11101
Email: info@ospreypublishing.com

© 2010 Osprey Publishing Ltd.

ISBN: 978 184603 919 5
ebook ISBN: 978 1 84908 271 6

Editor: Martin Windrow
Page layout by: Ken Vail Graphic Design, Cambridge, UK (kvgd.com)
Index by Mike Parkin
Typeset in Sabon and Myriad Pro
Originated by PDQ Media, Bungay, UK
Printed in China through Worldprint Ltd

10 11 12 13 14 10 9 8 7 6 5 4 3 2 1

A CIP catalog record for this book is available from the British Library

ACKNOWLEDGEMENTS

The author would like to thank the following individuals and institutions
whose assistance and support made this work possible: John A. Tilley
and Robert M. Browning, US Coast Guard Historian's Office; C. Kay Larson,
National Historian, USCG Aux; Anthony Bomba, Ensign, USN; Dorothy
(Dottie) Riley, District Staff Officer - Publications, USCG Aux; US Coast
Guard Museum; US National Archives; The Company of Military Historians;
and the members of Flotilla 79, 7th District, USCG Aux.

ARTIST'S NOTE

Readers may care to note that the original paintings from which the
color plates in this book were prepared are available for private sale.
All reproduction copyright whatsoever is retained by the Publishers.
All inquiries should be addressed to:

www.stephenwalshillustrations.co.uk

The Publishers regret that they can enter into no correspondence upon
this matter.

THE WOODLAND TRUST

Osprey Publishing is supporting the Woodland Trust, the UK's leading
woodland conservation charity, by funding the dedication of trees.

FOR A CATALOG OF ALL BOOKS PUBLISHED BY OSPREY MILITARY
AND AVIATION PLEASE CONTACT:

Osprey Direct, c/o Random House Distribution Center,
400 Hahn Road, Westminster, MD21157
E-mail: uscustomerservice@ospreypublishing.com

Osprey Direct, The Book Service Ltd, Distribution Centre,
Colchester Road, Frating Green, Colchester, Essex, CO7 7DW
E-mail: customerservice@ospreypublishing.com

www.ospreypublishing.com

CONTENTS

THE US COAST GUARD IN WORLD WAR II

INTRODUCTION

Some among those who study the enormous canvas of World War II operations are aware of the United States Coast Guard's part in the worldwide conflict, but for decades this has been obscured by the greater role played by its larger maritime sister service, the United States Navy.

The Coast Guardsmen or "coasties" live by their motto *Semper Paratus* – "Always Ready" – whether in times of peace or of war. While their conditions have changed depending upon the needs of the nation, their primary mission has remained the same – to serve as the United States' primary life-saving service on the seas and waterways. But the Coast Guard is also unique among the armed services in the degree to which it is multi-tasked, being a law-enforcement agency as well as a military force.

In a book of this size it is impossible to cover in detail all aspects of the service provided by the Coast Guard during World War II; however, it is hoped that this basic introduction to the subject may serve as a primer for others to pursue further research that will create a greater awareness of this often-overlooked subject. The simplest arithmetic speaks for itself as the justification for such an effort: during the war Coast Guardsmen manned – in addition to their own 800-plus cutters – some 640 other ships for the US Navy and US Army, and thousands of small landing craft; they fought at sea and in the air; they saved more than 4,000 lives during active operations, and were awarded nearly 2,000 decorations.

THE PRE-WAR COAST GUARD

The Coast Guard's predecessor, the Revenue Cutter Service, was founded on August 4, 1790, when the Tariff Act permitted construction of ten cutters and recruitment of 100 revenue officers. From 1790, when the Continental Navy was disbanded, until 1798, when the United States Navy was created, the Revenue Cutter Service provided the only armed American presence at sea. Revenue Marine cutters were involved in the Quasi-War with Revolutionary France in 1798–99, in the War of 1812 against Britain, in the Second Seminole War, the Mexican-American War, the Civil War, and the Spanish-American War.

In 1915 the US Revenue Cutter Service and the US Life Saving Service were combined by law to form the United States Coast Guard. It was provided that

the Coast Guard should constitute a part of the United States military forces, but that it should operate under the Treasury Department in time of peace; in time of war, or otherwise when the president should so direct, the Coast Guard functions as a part of the naval service. In the 1920s the Coast Guard was given several former US Navy four-stack destroyers to help enforce Prohibition. Although this effort was less than successful due to the slowness of the destroyers, the mission nevertheless provided many Coast Guard officers and petty officers with operational experience that proved invaluable during World War II. The Navy insult "Hooligan Navy" dates from this era, due to the Coast Guard's flexibility in enlisting men discharged from other services in order to expand its ranks rapidly; the epithet has endured due to the high proportion of prior members of other services among enlisted personnel, and has become a term of pride within the service.

On June 30, 1932, the Steamboat Inspection Service was merged with the Bureau of Navigation, itself created in 1884 to oversee the regulation of merchant seamen. On July 1, 1939, the Lighthouse Service became part of the Coast Guard. Following the outbreak of war in Europe in 1939 the Coast Guard carried out neutrality patrols, as set out by President Franklin D. Roosevelt on

September 5 of that year. Port security duties began on June 22, 1940, when President Roosevelt invoked the Espionage Act of 1917; this governed the anchorage and movement of all ships in US waters and protected American ships, harbors and waters. Shortly afterwards, the Dangerous Cargo Act gave the Coast Guard jurisdiction over ships carrying high explosives and other hazardous materials. In March 1941 the Coast Guard seized 28 Italian, two German and 35 Danish merchant ships. A few days later, ten modern Coast Guard cutters were transferred on Lend-Lease to Great Britain.

THE COAST GUARD RESERVE AND AUXILIARY

With the prospect of war approaching, Congress deemed it necessary to augment the US Coast Guard with a civilian reserve force. On June 23, 1939, Congress passed Title 14 of the United States Code establishing the US Coast Guard Reserve: "In the interest of (a) safety to life at sea and upon the navigable waters, (b) the promotion of efficiency in the operation of motorboats and yachts, and (c) a wider knowledge of, and better compliance with, the laws, rules, and regulations governing the operation and navigation of motorboats and yachts, and (d) facilitating certain operations of the Coast Guard, there is hereby established a United States Coast Guard Reserve... which shall be composed of citizens of the United States and its Territories and possessions... who are owners (sole or in part) of motorboats or yachts...."

This organization would be administered by the Commandant of the US Coast Guard, and was composed of unpaid, volunteer US citizens who owned suitable vessels. The new Coast Guard Reserve was originally meant to be a civilian organization; initially, members were not to hold military ranks, wear uniforms, receive military training, or "be vested with or exercise any right, privilege, power, or duty vested in or imposed upon the personnel of the Coast Guard." Reservists were invited to place their boats at the disposal of the Coast Guard "in the conduct of duties incident to the saving of life and property and in the patrol of marine parades and regattas," with the understanding that each such boat would be commanded by a regular Coast Guard officer or petty officer. Nor were Coast Guard Reservists to be considered government employees. Apart from a provision that "appropriations for the Coast Guard

A young Auxiliarist of the Coast Guard Auxiliary in khakis, demonstrating his skills with signal flags. Note the dark blue USCG shield just visible on the forearms of his shirt, and the brown leather boat shoes. (AdeQHA)

shall be available for the payment of actual necessary expenses of operation of any such motorboat or yacht when so utilized" (i.e., the Coast Guard would pay for the gas), it was expected that the Reserve would cost the government no money whatsoever. The Coast Guard would administer the Reserve through a regular officer with the title Chief Director of the Reserve, whose office would be in Washington, assisted by 14 District Directors.

The response in both the Coast Guard and the civilian boating community was, however, remarkably enthusiastic. By June 1940 Cdr Merlin O'Neill, the first Chief Director, and his District Directors had enrolled 2,600 men and 2,300 boats in the Coast Guard Reserve. With the support of USCG Commandant Russell R. Waesche, Coast Guard bases began offering training courses for reservists, and those who passed were appointed to three "reserve grades": senior navigator, navigator, and engineer.

In its original form the Coast Guard Reserve lasted less than two years. By early 1941 the Coast Guard was preparing for the United States' apparently inevitable entry into World War II, and events in Europe had demonstrated what demands on manpower and boats the service could expect to confront. On February 19, 1941, Congress passed a law restructuring the Coast Guard Reserve, and henceforth the USCG was to operate two distinct reserve forces. The existing civilian reserve organization was renamed the United States Coast Guard Auxiliary. A new US Coast Guard Reserve was to function on a military basis as a source of wartime manpower, like the reserves of the other armed services.

THE COAST GUARD GOES TO WAR

Pearl Harbor

At the time of the Japanese attack on Pearl Harbor, Coast Guard vessels in service in Hawaii were the 327ft cutter *Taney*, the 190ft buoy tender *Kukui*, two 125ft patrol craft (*Reliance* and *Tiger*), two 78ft patrol boats (CG-400 and CG-403), and several smaller craft. When the Japanese air strikes began the *Taney* was tied up at Pier 6 in Honolulu Harbor, *Reliance* and the unarmed *Kukui* both lay at Pier 4, and *Tiger* was on patrol along the western shore of Oahu. All were performing the normal duties for a peacetime Sunday.

ABOVE
Short of small craft, the Navy Department used the Coast Guard to procure more than 2,000 such vessels, most of them from Auxiliary members. This coastal picket fleet, mostly sailing yachts with a scattering of motor cruisers, cooperated closely with naval vessels and aircraft. The offshore duty could be punishing on vessels and crews, but large numbers were sent out to keep watch for Axis submarines running on the surface. By the end of the war some 5,000 Temporary Reservists had served in the "Corsair Fleet." This volunteer wears standard Navy-issue "dixie-cup" hat, chambray shirt and denim trousers. (USCG Historian's Office)

RIGHT
Formation of Coast Guard Auxiliarists serving in the Coast Guard Reserve (Temporary), who freed regular Coast Guardsmen for sea service by taking over Stateside duties such as port security. For uniform details, compare with Plates B4 and C3; note white USCG shield on forearms. (AdeQHA)

The Coast Guard's pre-war experience with African Americans differed from that of the other branches of the naval establishment. Unlike the Marine Corps but like the Navy, the Coast Guard could boast a tradition of black enlistment stretching far back to the previous century. Unlike the Navy, however, the USCG had always severely restricted both the numbers enlisted and the jobs assigned. Some 2,300 served in the racially separate Steward's Branch of the Coast Guard, performing the same duties in officers' messes and quarters as stewards in the Navy and Marine Corps, but the size of Coast Guard vessels and their crews necessitated the use of stewards at more important battle stations. In one case a group of stewards under the leadership of a black gun captain manned the 3in gun on the afterdeck of the cutter CGC *Campbell,* and won a citation for helping to destroy a U-boat in February 1943. The Personnel Division worked to make the separate Steward's Branch equal to the rest of the service in terms of promotion and pay, and individual stewards successfully applied for ratings in general service. The evidence suggests, however, that about 63 percent of all the black stewards in the USCG continued to function as servants throughout the war. Note, left, the distinctive cap insignia – see Plate H3. (AdeQHA)

After the first Japanese aircraft appeared over the island, USCGC *Taney*'s crew went to general quarters and made preparations to get underway but, while observing the attack over Pearl Harbor, they received no orders. At just after 9am, when the second wave of planes began their attack on the naval anchorage, *Taney* fired on high-altitude enemy aircraft with her 3in guns and .50cal machine guns, but due to the extreme range her guns had limited effect and were secured after 20 minutes.

Elsewhere, the patrolling CGC *Tiger* intercepted a dispatch from the USS *Ward* that claimed the destruction of an enemy submarine. Thirty-five minutes later, near Barber's Point, the cutter detected an underwater object on its rudimentary sonar apparatus, but lost the contact and resumed her patrol; she continued eastward toward the entrance of Pearl Harbor and, at around 8am, the crew were surprised to come under fire from an undetermined source, with shot falling within 100 yards. Lieutenant Mazzoni called his crew to general quarters and observed Japanese planes heading southwest away from Pearl Harbor; he manned the antiaircraft guns, but ordered no return fire because

of the extreme range. The *Tiger* immediately headed for her designated wartime station off the entrance to Honolulu Harbor; for the remainder of the morning she lay off the entrance, watching the air attacks from out of range and helpless to add her defensive fire. While the *Tiger* maintained her patrol off the harbor entrance during the night of December 7/8 she came under fire from understandably anxious Army units along the shore.

* * *

When war came to the United States the Coast Guard – in accordance with the statute of 1915 – was already operating as part of the US Navy. That law removed the service from the control of the Treasury Department during wartime or "at such time as the President shall direct," and this direction had been given on November 1, 1941. Henceforth the USCG would be subject to the orders of the Secretary of the Navy until January 1, 1946.

UNIFORMS

During World War I the United States Coast Guard rank structure became identical with that of the US Navy. At the time the highest rank in the Coast Guard was commodore, a rank reserved for the Commandant of the service; however, with the growth of the Coast Guard a higher rank was authorized, and the Commandant now holds the rank of vice admiral.

During the half-century between World War I and the Vietnam War the Coast Guard followed closely the uniform regulations of the US Navy, with the exception of devices used to distinguish between the two services. Commissioned officers of the Coast Guard wear a cap emblem consisting of a gold spread eagle with a silver shield superimposed on the breast, the talons grasping the shank of a silver fouled anchor with a gold cable. Warrant officers wear two crossed gold fouled anchors with a silver shield placed upright at their junction. Chief petty officers wear an upright gold fouled anchor upon which is superimposed a silver shield.

In addition, officers wear a gold embroidered United States shield above their sleeve rings of rank and on shoulder boards in place of the five-pointed star for Navy line officers. Enlisted men wear an embroidered shield on the right sleeve of the jumper midway between the cuff and the elbow; the shield is dark navy blue on white jumpers and white on blue jumpers. Chief petty officers with gold rating badges wear a gold embroidered shield, and CPOs wearing silver rating badges display the shield embroidered in silver.

The only special uniform the Coast Guard inventoried prior to World War II was the Surfman's uniform, worn by men of the Lifeboat stations. As the Lifeboat stations were "integrated" with the regular sailors from the cutter fleet early in World War II, the rating of surfman was abolished in 1942, along with the special uniform.

A Coast Guard Warrant Officer in dress whites. Chief Warrant Officers in the Coast Guard might be found in command of larger small-boat stations and patrol boats, and as specialists and supervisors in other technical areas; under magnification this man's shoulder boards show the specialty rating consisting of crossed anchors, identifying him as a Boatswain. (AdeQHA)

In May 1942 the Secretary of the Navy authorized uniforms for the Coast Guard Auxiliary. These were based on those worn by the regular Coast Guard, but with distinctive insignia for the Auxiliarists. Temporary Members of the Auxiliary were authorized a uniform resembling that of the Surfmen except for insignia.

At first a division under the Chief of Naval Operations, the headquarters of the Coast Guard was later granted considerably more administrative autonomy. On February 28, 1942, Executive Order 9083 transferred the Bureau of Marine Inspection temporarily to the Coast Guard under Navy Department control. In March 1942, Secretary Knox carefully delineated the Navy's control over the Coast Guard, making the Chief of Naval Operations responsible for the operation of those Coast Guard ships, aircraft and stations assigned to the naval commands for the "proper conduct of the war," but

A member of the USCG Women's Reserve – the "SPARs" – that provided logistical services to the Coast Guard. This petty officer second class holds a rating of radioman/radio technician. Note the distinctive jacket collar – see Plate F1. (AdeQHA)

specifying that assignments be made with "due regard for the needs of the Coast Guard," which must continue to carry out its regular functions. Such duties as providing port security, ice-breaking services, and navigational aid remained under the direct control and supervision of the Commandant, the local naval district commander exercising only "general military control" of these activities in his area. The Coast Guard also retained administrative control over the recruitment, training, and assignment of personnel. Like the US Marine Corps, it also had a staff agency for manpower planning (the Commandant's Advisory Board), and one for administration (the Personnel Division), which were independent of the Navy's bureaus.

USCG Women's Reserve

On November 23, 1942, Congress enacted Public Law 773, which established a Women's Reserve as a branch of the Coast Guard. Members of this branch became known as SPARs, an acronym drawn from the service's motto *Semper Paratus*. The SPARs mainly replaced men in shore stations, working in

A pair of SPARs working with a Coast Guard aviator. He has his USCG officer's emblem on his overseas cap. The US Navy and USMC flying jacket G-1 (also called AN-J-3A), made of goatskin leather, replaced the M-422A in 1943. Although generally similar to the USAAF A-2 jacket it had different details: a fur collar, a storm flap behind the zipper (punched with the letters "USN"), a bi-swing back panel with a half-belt, and button-through flaps on the two patch pockets. In 1932, Coast Guard Air Station Miami was commissioned at Dinner Key, and became the first "contemporary" aviation unit in the US Coast Guard, flying a variety of fixed-wing amphibians. These early fliers were tasked with routine coastal patrols, search-and-rescue (both maritime and aviation-related), and the interdiction of smugglers. With the outbreak of World War II the Coast Guard pilots from Miami flew antisubmarine warfare and convoy support missions in addition to the station's primary function as a military search-and-rescue asset. During the war the Coast Guard operated PBY, PBM, JRF and OS2U seaplanes from Dinner Key. (AdeQHA)

traditional clerical and other routine duties. As the war progressed, however, Coast Guard women were placed in charge of greater areas of previously male-only control. This led, for example, to a small group of SPARs working in the field of Coast Guard aviation as parachute-riggers, link trainer operators, aviation machinists' mates and air control tower operators. Others worked as radio technicians, gunners' mates or radar operators. The SPARs' successful performance of vital administrative and organizational functions extended their duty from purely clerical tasks, as first envisioned, to the most important port security, logistical and administrative jobs by war's end. By D-Day on June 6, 1944, when the Allies landed to liberate German-held France, the SPARs contained 771 officers and 7,600 enlisted servicewomen. In addition, the Coast Guard's medical service was already composed of Public Health Service nurses and even female PHS medical officers on direct combat and shipboard assignments.

THE HOME FRONT

To help guard against the perceived increasing threat of enemy saboteurs, and to make up for a lack of sufficient coastal patrols, the Coast Guard, after approval by Congress, established a program similar to the Local Defence Volunteers (later to be known as the Home Guard) in Great Britain.[1] Qualified volunteer individuals or entire units would be assigned as Temporary Members of the US Coast Guard Reserve, and many Auxiliarists were commissioned as

1 This was not a paranoid overreaction. The German submarines U-202 and U-584 did land two parties of saboteurs on the coasts of Long Island and Florida; and Japanese submarines I-17, I-25, and I-26 did shell West Coast targets in 1942. See Elite 161: *The US Home Front 1941–45*.

Temporary Reservists providing port security; note (right) the "USCG/ TR" shoulder patch and "COAST/ GUARD/ POLICE" armband. The wartime history of Port Security, USCG Seattle, noted: "On August 4, 1942, the District Coast Guard Officer, 13th Naval District, was directed by Headquarters to enroll, as a special group of Temporary Reservists, private plant guards in facilities where… construction of interest to the Navy was being carried out. The primary purpose of the establishment of the Coast Guard Police was to give the facilities involved a certain amount of military protection, large military immunity, and the law enforcement power of the Coast Guard." (USCG Historian's Office)

temporary officers of the Coast Guard Reserve (TRs). Members of the new Coast Guard Reserve were to be divided into two categories. "Regular Reservists" were paid for their services, had to meet normal military physical standards, and when on active duty could be assigned to stations anywhere the Coast Guard deemed appropriate. Men who, for any reason, were unable to meet those requirements were invited to become "Temporary Members of the Reserve." A Coast Guard "TR" was a volunteer who served only in some designated geographic area (usually near his home or workplace) and less than full time. Age limits for TRs were set generously, between 17 and 74 years, and physical requirements were not stringent. Members of the renamed Auxiliary were invited to enroll in the Reserve as TRs, and to bring their boats with them. (Additionally, some 2,000 women enrolled as "TR SPARs," attending to the mountainous paperwork generated by the dispatch of ships, cargoes, and troops overseas.)

A THE EARLY DAYS, 1939–42

1: USCG CAPTAIN, FULL DRESS

Prior to the United States' entry into World War II the Coast Guard had long followed the basic uniform practice of the United States Navy; this captain is wearing the full dress uniform of the late 1930s. The black felt bicorn hat is trimmed with black silk and gold lace. The frock coat has two rows of five gilt buttons, fringed gold lace epaulets, and for this rank four gold cuff rings surmounted by the USCG shield on both sleeves; this veteran officer displays the Navy Cross and the 1918 Victory Medal. The Coast Guard officer's sword differs from that of Navy officers in having "USCG" instead of "USN" on the hilt and a Coast Guard shield on the scabbard throat.

2: VICE ADMIRAL RUSSELL R. WAESCHE, USCG COMMANDANT; SERVICE BLUES

Vice Admiral Waesche wears the standard blue service uniform, with the characteristic "reefer" coat worn by officers of all ranks of the maritime services. It has two rows of three gilt buttons, and is distinguished here only by the gold-embroidered USCG shield above the three medium and one wide gold lace cuff rings denoting rank.

3. USCG WARRANT OFFICER, WHITE SERVICE DRESS

Service blues can be worn the year round, but white service dress normally during the summer or in tropical stations. Note the characteristic "sit" of the cap and the emblem of this rank (see Plate H5); the standing collar, two breast pockets and single row of five buttons on the jacket; and the WO's shoulder boards, here with the emblem of the Supply Branch.

Each TR, even though on unpaid duty status with the Coast Guard, was a member of the armed forces of the United States of America. All were required to swear allegiance to the USA, and all were subject to military discipline and punishment under the Uniform Code of Military Justice (UCMJ). The question of arming the Temporary Reserves and their boats rested with the local Coast Guard unit commander or officer-in-charge. (Note that the now-renamed Coast Guard Auxiliary – the pre-February 1941 "Reserve" – remained a non-military, unarmed service. Confusingly, when Auxiliarists were on duty as Temporary Reserves, they were no longer Auxiliarists but military personnel; as soon as they went off duty, they returned to Auxiliary status.)

Port security and beach patrol

Perhaps the Auxiliary's most important contribution to the war effort came in the form of the Volunteer Port Security Force. An executive order of February 1942 directed the Secretary of the Navy to take the necessary steps to prevent "sabotage and subversive activities" on the nation's waterfronts. The task of protecting the hundreds of warehouses, piers, and other facilities that kept the American shipping industry in business fell to the Coast Guard, which in turn delegated it to the Reserve and the Auxiliary. In every port city within the United States there was a Coast Guard officer with the title of Captain of the Port, who was placed in charge of a Port Security Force consisting of TRs, Auxiliarists, and other civilians recruited for the purpose. The precise organizational structure varied from city to city. The Coast Guard set up a Reserve Training School in Philadelphia to train TRs in such skills as anti-espionage methods, fire prevention, customs inspections, and small-arms handling. Eventually some 20,000 Reservists and Auxiliarists participated in port security patrols.

The Beach Patrol program began on October 12, 1942. The Coast Guard's job was to patrol shorelines and alert the Army to any possible dangers, and to this end both horse and dog patrols were established along with a network of watchtowers. In Florida, for instance, the 45 bridges spanning the Inland Waterway were guarded from St Augustine to Key West, and the Coast Guard checked both land and sea traffic. By spring 1943 there were 2,000 men on duty in this 7th Naval District, along with 200 dogs and 500 horses. The foot patrols covered about 12 miles of beaches every night, and the mounted patrols about 20 miles. Horses were authorized for the US Coast Guard Beach Patrol program in September 1942, and the mounted element soon became the majority, with 3,222 horses by September 1943. The horses and riding gear were provided by the Army Remount Service, while the Coast Guard provided the uniforms. A call went out for personnel, and a mixed bag of people responded – polo-players, cowboys, former sheriffs, horse trainers, Army Reserve cavalrymen, jockeys, farm boys, rodeo riders and stunt men. Although they worked mostly in pairs the Coast Guard cavalrymen were also trained to work in units. Much of the mounted training took place at Elkins Park Training Station and Hilton Head, the sites of the dog-training schools.

As the war ground on and the Coast Guard's resources were stretched thinner, Auxiliarists and TRs were called upon to fill gaps wherever active duty Coast Guardsmen left them. Auxiliarists' boats patrolled the waterfronts and inlets looking for saboteurs, enemy agents, and fires. At least one unit of Temporary Reservists, recruited from the Auxiliary, patrolled east coast beaches on horseback. Other Auxiliarists manned lookout and lifesaving stations near their homes, freeing regular Coast Guardsmen for sea duty. When a flood struck St Louis in the spring of 1943, Coast Guard Auxiliarists and Reservists evacuated 7,000 people and thousands of head of livestock.

By the end of the war the Coast Guard Auxiliary boasted a membership of 67,533, of which 53,214 men and women were serving as Temporary Members of the Reserve. At the end of hostilties the Coast Guard TRs were "honorably disenrolled," though many remained Auxiliarists for years afterward. Wartime service had earned them no veterans' benefits and precious little other public recognition. In 1946 the TRs were awarded the Victory Medal, but Auxiliarists who had not joined the Reserve had to be satisfied with the thanks of Adm Waesche: "The Auxiliary during the war years was indispensable. Many thousands of you served faithfully and loyally as Auxiliarists and as temporary members of the CG Reserve, performing hundreds of tasks and relieving thousands of Coast Guardsmen for duty outside the continental limits. The Coast Guard is deeply appreciative of this service."

ABOVE
Beginning in 1942, the Coast Guard eventually received about 2,000 dogs for patrol duties. Many dogs and their handlers were schooled on the 300-acre estate of P.A.B. Widener, at the Elkin Park Training Station in Pennsylvania; others trained at Hilton Head, South Carolina. The first dog patrols began at Brigantine Park, New Jersey, in August 1942; they were so successful that within a year dog-handlers were on duty in all the USCG districts. Note the Reising submachine gun – see also Plate C4. (USCG Historian's Office)

LEFT
The Vought OS2U Kingfisher, a scout and observation floatplane, entered service with the Navy in August 1940; it could be fitted with a removable undercarriage and tail wheel for handling while on land. Beginning in March 1942, the Coast Guard eventually acquired 53 Kingfishers of both the OS2U-2 and OS2U-3 models, the OS2U-3 having extra fuel tanks and better armor protection for the crew. The Kingfishers carried the burden of the Coast Guard's early antisubmarine efforts along the nation's coastlines and in coastal waters, and scouted for coastal merchant convoys. They were capable of carrying a depth charge and could fly patrols lasting up to six hours; none of the Coast Guard-operated floatplanes were credited with sinking an enemy submarine, but many made rescues of survivors from torpedoed merchant ships. (AdeQHA)

THE BATTLE OF THE ATLANTIC

The first combats between the armed forces of the United States and Nazi Germany were occasioned by Adm Karl Doenitz's relentless U-boat campaign to sever the ocean supply lines between America, Great Britain, and the Soviet Union. These sea lanes fed and equipped the Allies and permitted the military build-up that led to the liberation of Europe, but until at least May 1943 the issue seemed to the Allies to remain in doubt. The Coast Guard's participation in this campaign has been generally overlooked; while the service continued its traditional lifesaving duties along the nation's shores during the war, its ships and aircraft ventured well out to sea, protecting convoys along the US coast and right across to Europe and Africa (and, indeed, in the Pacific).

Coast Guard operations in the North Atlantic began before the United States entered the war, and included neutrality and weather-patrol cruises. The Coast Guard also began operations in Greenland, a Danish colony, soon after Denmark fell to the Germans in 1940, and on April 9, 1941 Greenland was incorporated into a hemispheric defense system. The Coast Guard was the primary military service responsible for these cold-weather operations, which continued throughout the war. On September 12, 1941 the cutter *Northland* took into "protective custody" the Norwegian trawler *Buskoe* and captured three German radiomen ashore – the United States' first naval capture of the war. By October 1941 all Coast Guard and Navy forces in Greenland waters were consolidated into a unified Greenland Patrol and placed under the command of Coast Guard Cdr Edward "Iceberg" Smith. The Patrol established bases, escorted convoys, destroyed German weather-reporting

---

B

US MARITIME AND LIGHTHOUSE SERVICES, 1939–41

1: USMS LIEUTENANT, 1941
The Merchant Marine Act, enacted by Congress on June 29, 1936, created the US Merchant Marine and the US Maritime Service, to "serve as a Naval or Military Auxiliary in time of war or national emergency." In 1938 the US Maritime Service was established "for the education and training of citizens… for the safe and efficient operation of the Merchant Marine of the United States at all times… The ranks, grades and ratings for the personnel of the US Maritime Service shall be the same as for the personnel of the US Coast Guard." During World War II the USMS was administered by the US Coast Guard and US Navy, and many young men were sent to the Maritime Service by both Navy and Coast Guard recruiters with the phrase, "That's where your services are needed." The USMS was the only service that did not discriminate racially. The naval-style officer's service blues are distinguished only by insignia (see Plate H6).

2: USMS TRAINEE, 1939
This is essentially the US Navy enlisted man's blue jumper working uniform, with a plain collar; the white tape around the right shoulder seam is the Seaman branch "watch mark" (engine-room personnel wore a red tape round the left shoulder). His service is immediately distinguishable by the red-on-blue USMS patch on his right upper sleeve.

3: USLHS LIGHTHOUSE KEEPER, 1939
The USLHS was created in 1910 as the successor to the Lighthouse Board; until it was merged with the Coast Guard in 1939 it had its own fleet of tenders, painted black (in contrast to Navy gray and Coast Guard white). This experienced old lighthouse keeper is illustrated as he appeared in the transitional phase, wearing a USCG lighthouse keeper's cap badge on his "train conductor"-style cap, with his old USLHS uniform. The reefer jacket has two rows of four buttons, and gold-edged collar patches with "K" for keeper.

4: USCG SURFMAN
The Surfman designation dated back to the creation of the Coast Guard in 1915, when the US Life Saving Service merged with the US Revenue Cutter Service. The surfmen manned the USLSS lifeboat stations around the country's coastline; to maintain their *esprit de corps* after the merger the Coast Guard soon authorized a special uniform for them, and this was kept on the books until at least 1943. The cap was the same as that authorized for chief petty officers except for the device: "brass, gold plated, fitted with a hinged clasp pin; crossed oars superimposed on a circular life buoy; oars to be about $1^3/8$ inches in length, crossed in the middle of the life buoy; life buoy to be about $3/4$ inch in diameter," all superimposed on a fouled anchor. The emblem minus the anchor (see Plate H5) was repeated on the peaked lapels of the military-style single-breasted tunic, which had four front buttons and four pockets; note the USCG shield on the right forearm.

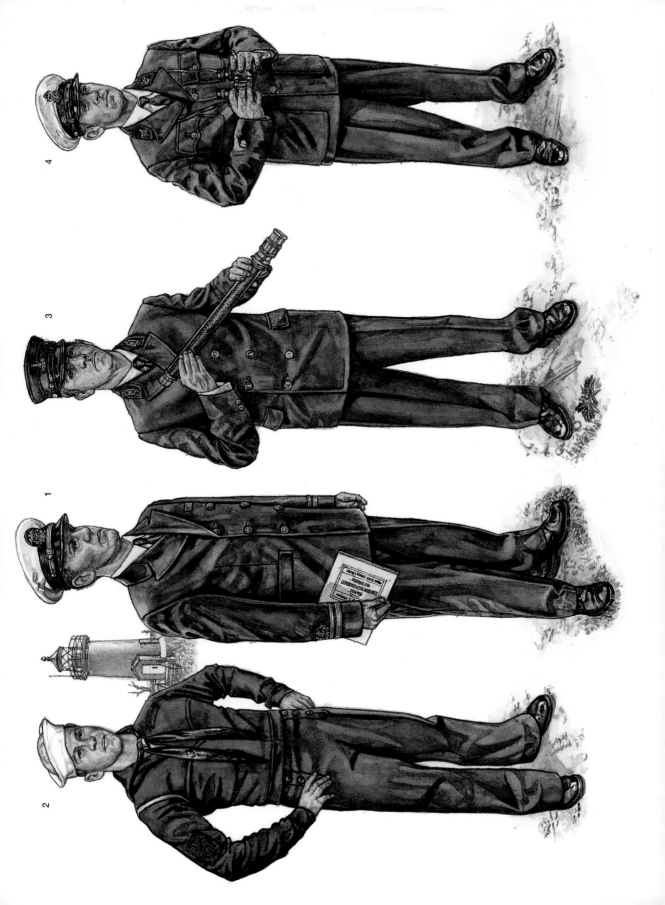

Northeastern Greenland: some of 12 Germans under guard by members of a landing party from a Coast Guard cutter that surprised and captured their weather-radio installation; soon afterwards the Coast Guard captured a German armed trawler in nearby icefields. During the summer and early fall of 1942 the Coast Guard captured approximately 60 Germans, destroyed two radio stations, forced the scuttling of a second trawler, and found a third abandoned in the ice. (AdeQHA)

radio stations, and rescued survivors from torpedoed ships. A Coast Guard-manned patrol bombing squadron, VPB-6, also operated over the North Atlantic from its home base in Greenland during the war.

Doenitz's "Drumbeat"

Although Adm Doenitz's relative weakness in available boats prevented him from taking full advantage of his opportunity in the days immediately following Pearl Harbor and Germany's declaration of war, by Christmas Day 1941 he had six submarines heading west across the Atlantic to open Operation *Paukenschlag* ("Drumbeat") against shipping in North American coastal waters, between the Gulf of St Lawrence and Cape Hatteras. These, and the boats that followed, were manned by some of the most combat-experienced submarine captains and crews in the world, and they found themselves in a happy hunting-ground.

United States shipping had not yet adopted a convoy system; vessels sailed individually, making free use of their radios, fully lit at night, and silhouetted from out to sea against the brilliantly illuminated backdrop of coastal cities where a blackout would not be fully in operation for another five months. During daylight hours the U-boats remained submerged, surfacing at nightfall to wreak havoc with torpedoes and deck guns; so innocent were the merchantmen that the first to be sunk, the tanker *Norness*, radioed that it had hit a mine, prompting a general warning against mines the next day. On some nights a U-boat might hope to claim three victims, with resulting immense Allied losses in supplies and munitions. In the space of just two weeks the first wave of U-boats sank 20 merchant ships totaling 150,000 tons, and during February 1942 nearly 70 ships were sunk.

At the time when the U-boat campaign against the United States began, available Coast Guard forces included 56 aircraft, seven relatively new 327ft Secretary-class cutters, eight other large cutters, 23x 165ft cutters, 31x 125ft cutters, plus a wide assortment of lightships, tenders, tugs, smaller patrol craft and lifeboats. Although many of the cutters dated from the days of Prohibition or even earlier, they proved to be effective escorts. Various smaller craft and other vessels were also commissioned into service as emergency acquisitions. A shortage of escorts, conflicting priorities in the allocation of those escorts, and poor planning combined to delay the introduction of a convoy system along the coast until May 1942. As the U-boats attacked the unescorted merchant ships many Coast Guard units, augmented by Reserve and Temporary Reserve vessels, rescued survivors and chased down suspected U-boat contacts.

Coast Guard cutters destroyed two long-range Type IX submarines off the American coastline during the latter days of this German offensive: the 165ft CGC *Icarus* sank U-352 (Kapitänleutnant Rathke) off North Carolina on

The backbone of the Coast Guard patrols off home shores at the time of America's entry into World War II were these patrol boats armed with a 3in (76mm) Mk 21 dual-purpose deck gun, water-cooled .50cal and air-cooled .30cal Lewis machine guns. (AdeQHA)

Posed shot of Coast Guard aviators supposedly rushing to their aircraft in the course of antisubmarine patrols along the Atlantic seaboard. The spring and early summer of 1942 was a time of heavy shipping losses in these under-protected sea lanes during Adm Doenitz's Operation "Drumbeat." (USCG Historian's Office)

May 9, 1942, and its sister cutter *Thetis* destroyed U-157 (Korvettenkapitän Henne) off Key West, Florida, on June 13. To put these successes in context, in the period December 1941–July 1942 a total of only six U-boats were sunk in American waters. Coast Guard aircraft made 61 unsuccessful bombing attacks on U-boat contacts by the end of summer 1942; they also sighted and reported the location of more than 1,000 survivors, and rescued 95.

The workhorses of the fleet, the Coast Guard's tenders and tugs, also kept the coastal trade routes open. Along the coast of Florida, for instance, they salvaged four torpedoed vessels that spring and summer of 1942. Tenders, such as the CGC *Juniper*, had the solemn task of marking the wrecks of ships sunk by U-boats as hazards to navigation. One tender, the CGC *Acacia*, fell victim herself when she was shelled and sunk by U-161 (Kapitänleutnant Achilles); the *Acacia* was the only Coast Guard tender lost to enemy action during the war, and fortunately her crew all survived.

When a convoy system for coastal shipping was finally established – initially in the area between Halifax, Nova Scotia, and New York – the new system deterred the U-boats, and ship losses declined. During summer of 1942 the U-boats left American waters in search of easier prey further south in the Caribbean and South Atlantic, although occasional forays by individual submarines continued to enforce vigilance on the escorts of coastal convoys, augmented by newly constructed 83ft patrol craft.

THE NORTH ATLANTIC

Six Secretary-class cutters were already escorting the western legs of North Atlantic open-ocean convoys prior to America's official entry into the war; the first to begin such duty was the CGC *Campbell*, which joined the escort for convoy HX-159 in November 1941. The CGC *Ingham* followed, and by

April 1942 four more had joined their sister cutters on the North Atlantic convoy routes. The dangerous nature of escort duty was made plain when the cutter *Alexander Hamilton* fell victim to a torpedo attack in January 1942, but the other five, alongside Navy destroyers, continued to be the mainstay of the American escort effort through mid-1943.

The Canadians, British, and Americans enjoyed a number of decisive advantages over the U-boats. Among these was a high-frequency radio direction-finder, HFDF or "huff-duff," which determined the bearings of radio transmissions. The Coast Guard had been involved with radio direction-finding since 1919 and had gained further experience by the use of both ship and shore-based stations while chasing rum-runners during Prohibition, and in 1941 the Coast Guard took over the operation of 22 shore-based stations in the United States from the Navy. Since German U-boat tactics called for centralized control of the submarines by radio, "huff-duff" paved the way to locating them based on their regular radio traffic. It took time, however, to notify convoys of bearings obtained by shore-based stations, so ship-based HFDF was critical. A convoy, notified almost instantaneously that a U-boat was nearby, could quickly change course to evade it, or send an escort vessel down the bearing of the radio signal to attack it. The escort, more heavily armed than a submarine, forced the U-boat to submerge and prevented it from directing more U-boats to the convoy's location. The CGC *Campbell* and *Spencer* had the distinction of being two of the first American warships equipped with ship-based "huff-duff" equipment.

Another and superlative advantage was, of course, "Ultra," the codename for the Allied effort to break Germany's military and naval radio ciphers. When the British, building upon original Polish expertise, succeeded in breaking those ciphers, and captured an example of the German "Enigma" coding machine from an abandoned and sinking submarine, they were able to plot the locations of U-boat "wolf packs" and route the convoys around them.

A typical posed shot, of a Coast Guardsman finding cheer in a cup of steaming coffee as he stands watch aboard a combat cutter in the biting cold of the North Atlantic. Exceptionally bad winter weather and mounting exhaustion made convoy escort duty in small warships one of the most physically punishing and nerve-racking of wartime assignments. (AdeQHA)

"Ultra" intelligence proved to be decisive, but there were blackouts in the flow of information when the Germans changed their ciphers, thereby depriving the Allies of this important resource until the cryptanalysts at Bletchley Park outside London could break the new cipher in its turn. Another problem complicated the picture: the Germans themselves broke Allied merchant shipping radio codes. With the information thus obtained they were able to determine the sailing routes of some convoys and accurately position wolf packs for interceptions. On these occasions, and others when the U-boats located a convoy simply through circumstance, the convoy escorts relied on ship-based "huff-duff"; on another Allied advantage – radar, which could locate submarines on the surface; and on aggressive escort tactics guided by sonar – underwater sound location.

Radar, such as the sets installed on the USCG cutters before they began escort duty, permitted Allied warships both to keep to their designated stations within the convoys during the frequent bad visibility in the North Atlantic, and – more importantly – to locate nearby surfaced U-boats. U-boat tactics depended on the ability to operate on the surface at night, moving faster and using their diesel engines to recharge their batteries, and – preferably – making surface torpedo attacks; when forced to submerge they had to use their electric motors, which cut their speed. Escorts tracked submerged U-boats with sonar, an acoustic location and ranging device that could rob the submarine of its most important advantage: the ability to hide beneath the ocean's surface. Once an escort located a submerged U-boat it attacked with depth charges, "hedgehog" mortars, or other antisubmarine weapons. However, maintaining contact with an evading submarine was a demanding skill; it took escort crews time and experience to learn how to employ these cutting-edge technologies and weapon systems to their fullest potential, and in the interim losses were consequently heavy.

Through March 1943 only one North Atlantic escort group, Ocean Escort Group A-3, was under American command, but the distinction was nominal because of the mingling of Allied navies in these groups. Group A-3, for instance, commanded by US Navy Capt Paul R. Heineman, initially consisted of the CGC *Spencer* and *Campbell*, and one British and four Canadian corvettes. Many warships were transferred between groups, and Group A-3, along with the others, was reinforced when under particular strain with escorts of various nationalities, or the Coast Guard cutters *Bibb*, *Duane*, and *Ingham*. These three Secretary-class cutters also escorted smaller convoys from the main convoy routes to Iceland and back again.

"The Bloody Winter"

Long-range aircraft were not assigned to convoy protection duties in sufficient numbers to cover the convoys across the entire width of the North Atlantic until the middle of 1943, and consequently there was an "air gap" south of Greenland. It was here that most of the ocean battles were waged, and the area

A US Coast Guard combat cutter on antisubmarine escort duties in the North Atlantic. Six of the Secretary-class cutters were assigned to this campaign, of which one was torpedoed and lost as early as January 1942. (AdeQHA)

earned the nicknames "Torpedo Junction" from the Allies and "Devil's Gorge" from the Germans. To make matters worse, weather along the North Atlantic convoy routes bordered on the hellish; in bad weather the heavy seas rendered radar and sonar practically useless, and the storms of winter 1942/43 were the worst to hit the North Atlantic in more than 50 years. This, in conjunction with a renewed U-boat offensive on the North Atlantic routes, led to that period being nicknamed the "Bloody Winter."

The cutters' first North Atlantic victory came when the *Ingham* (Cdr George E. McCabe) located a submerged U-boat while screening ahead of Convoy SC-112 on the night of December 17, 1942. The *Ingham* attacked, laying depth charges at varying depths to create what McCabe called a "hammer effect." Aboard the cutter deck plates rattled as the charges exploded, sending vast fountains of seawater and spray skyward; finally they found their mark, and the U-626 (Lt Hans-Botho Bade) went to the bottom with all hands. In January 1943 the weather was so bad that the U-boats had difficulty locating and attacking convoys, but by February more than 100 were stationed in the "air gap," and even with the intelligence provided by "Ultra" the Allies could not evade so many. They wreaked havoc among the merchant ships during February, and the escorts were kept busy both attempting to track the enemy and pulling desperate survivors from the water.

One such rescue typified the Coast Guard's role during that "Bloody Winter." During the night of February 3/4, 1943, U-233 torpedoed and sank the troop-carrying passenger ship SS *Dorchester*, bound for Greenland. Its escorts from the Greenland Patrol – the CGC *Tampa*, *Escanaba*, and *Comanche*, later supported by the CGC *Duane* – worked in the icy darkness to try to save survivors; they rescued 229 of the 904 passengers and crew, but the frigid waters claimed the rest. This rescue was the first recorded use of the "retriever" technique, by which a crewman, insulated against the lethally cold water by a rubber suit and tethered to the ship, was lowered into the sea to attempt to grab a survivor. Crewmen aboard would then haul both in, recover the survivor, and throw the rescuer back in to retrieve another.

Another rescue demonstrated the brutal nature of combat in the North Atlantic when a wolf pack attacked the eastbound convoy SC-118, to whose Royal Navy escort group the USCG cutters *Bibb* and *Ingham* had been

Even before the war Coast Guardsmen were quite accustomed to the extreme conditions of the North Atlantic and Bering Straits, but in the heavy storms of the winter 1942/43 the constant rolling and pitching of such small warships as the USCG cutters and British and Canadian corvettes added greatly to the exhaustion of crews forced to remain alert at all times to the threat of the lurking U-boats. These "coasties" bracing themselves against the rolling of a cutter in heavy seas are wearing typical cold-weather clothing, including the fur-lined N-1 winter parka, bib-front padded overtrousers and cloth-and-rubber overshoes – see Plate E1. (AdeQHA)

temporarily attached. Straggling behind the convoy, the troopship SS *Henry Mallory* was torpedoed by U-402 (KK Siegfried Freiherr von Forstner). The passengers panicked and leapt overboard, and those who did not manage to struggle to a life raft quickly died from hypothermia. Lookouts aboard the *Bibb* sighted one of the *Mallory's* lifeboats and, ignoring an order to return to the convoy, Cdr Roy Raney ordered his crew to begin a rescue attempt. Many of the *Bibb's* crewmen leapt into the water to assist the nearly frozen survivors, and the cutter *Ingham* assisted. Although many of the *Henry Mallory's* 498 passengers and crew perished, the *Bibb* saved 202 survivors and the *Ingham* another 33; the *Bibb's* crew also rescued 33 more men from the nearby torpedoed freighter SS *Kalliopi* before returning to the convoy.

Escort Group A-3: the battle for ON-166

The fighting in "Torpedo Junction" worsened as the winter dragged on, and one of the fiercest battles was waged over Convoy ON-166 in February 1943. This westbound convoy was under the protection of Escort Group A-3, whose Capt Heineman flew his flag aboard the CGC *Spencer*, commanded by Coast Guard Cdr Harold S. Berdine. The cutter *Campbell* (Coast Guard Cdr James A. Hirshfield) also sailed with this international escort group, which became more so with the arrival in reinforcement of the Free Polish destroyer *Burza*.

ON-166 left the waters off Northern Ireland and sailed straight into a gale, and as the high seas tossed the ships about, disrupting their formation, no fewer than 21 U-boats closed in to attack. Hirshfield noted with alarm the number of HFDF contacts, and commented that the convoy was certainly "in for a big party." On the night of February 20/21 the *Spencer* located U-604 (KL Horst Höltring) on radar. It dived as the cutter closed in, and the *Spencer* laced the water with depth charges; although Höltring managed to evade successfully, he had been prevented from reporting the convoy's position.

The following night the *Spencer* again obtained a radar contact and sailed to investigate, and as the range closed the Coast Guard crew spotted a submarine motoring on the surface. The U-boat crash-dived, but the *Spencer* established sonar contact almost immediately; this time the depth charges were right on target, and U-529 (KL Georg-Werner Fraatz) went to the bottom with all hands.

The *Campbell* was also kept busy that night; she obtained several radar contacts, forcing U-boats to submerge and damaging at least two. Her crew then rescued 50 survivors from a torpedoed Norwegian tanker, and as the cutter steamed to catch up with the convoy again it detected yet another surfaced submarine. The *Campbell* raced toward it and soon made visual contact; it was U-606 (Olt Hans Döhler), earlier disabled and forced to the surface by depth charges from the *Burza*. The *Campbell* closed to ram while her gunners opened fire, but the big cutter struck the U-boat only a glancing

Convoy HX-233, April 16, 1943: steaming between the columns of merchant ships, Coast Guardsmen on the stern of the cutter *Spencer* watch the explosion of the depth charges that foiled the submerged daylight attack by U-175. (AdeQHA)

blow and one of the submarine's hydroplanes sliced open the *Campbell*'s hull, flooding the engine room. The crew dropped two depth charges as the submarine slid past, and the explosions lifted the U-boat nearly five feet. The *Campbell* illuminated the U-boat with a searchlight and the gunners continued to fire into the submarine's conning tower and hull; Cdr Hirshfield was hit by shell fragments but remained at his station. When he realized that the Germans had given up he ordered his men to cease firing, and they then rescued five of the U-606's crew of about 60 all ranks. The U-606 was finished, but so was the *Campbell* for the immediate future; the cutter was dead in the water with a flooded engine room. Hirshfield directed the repairs while the *Burza*, and later a British corvette, screened his wallowing ship from any attack. A tug arrived nearly four days later and towed the crippled cutter to Newfoundland; the *Campbell* was later repaired and returned to service.

The battle for ON-166 was far from over, however, and with the *Campbell* out of action the now weakened Group A-3 continued to fight off attacking U-boats. The *Spencer* located the submerged U-454 (KL Klaus Hackländer) as it attempted to attack the convoy, and depth-charged it so severely that it was forced out of the action. The battle wound down as the convoy neared Newfoundland; it had lasted nearly a week, and had been fought over 1,000 miles of the winter ocean.

Convoy SC-121: fighting blind

March 1943 proved to be one of the most devastating months of the Atlantic war for the Allies. The Germans changed their Kriegsmarine radio cipher, depriving the Allies of precious "Ultra" intelligence, and during the first three weeks of the month they lost 97 ships – at that rate even American industrial production could not keep up with losses. There was little rest for the desperately needed Coast Guard cutters in the North Atlantic, with consequent breakdowns in equipment due to a lack of time for repairs (the *Ingham* sailed with inoperative sonar for nearly six weeks before being permitted to go into dry dock). The crews, too, were exhausted by their relentless duty in the storms of "the Bloody Winter."

In early March, Escort Group A-3 sailed east toward Great Britain escorting 59 ships of Convoy SC-121 through a winter gale. Again, despite the heavy seas U-boats closed in to attack; the storm dispersed many of the merchant ships, allowing the subs to pick off the stragglers. The CGC *Spencer* attacked and drove off at least four submarines, but the cutter and the few corvettes became overwhelmed; Capt Heineman requested reinforcements,

A boat party from CGC *Spencer* boarding the crippled U-175 after KL Heinrich Bruns was forced to bring his boat to the surface. Coast Guard Lt Ross Bullard became the first American to board an enemy "man-of-war underway at sea" since the War of 1812. (USCG Historian's Office)

The crew of U-175 were extraordinarily lucky, in that all 41 men were picked up safely from the calm, daylight sea; most actions took place at night, and anyway a lost U-boat normally took all hands to the bottom. This survivor was identified as a petty officer, Obersteurmann Helmut Klotzch. (USCG Historian's Office)

and soon the *Bibb* and *Ingham* departed Iceland and headed out to sea in support. The heavy seas continued to disperse the convoy; even with the escort reinforced, seven of the stragglers were sunk by U-boats, and six more while within the convoy. Much of the escorts' sonar and radar equipment was inoperative due to the heavy seas or lack of timely maintenance and repairs, which accounted for the lack of U-boat kills. However, under Capt Heineman's direction the escorts' counterattacks kept the U-boats from sinking even more merchantmen. Convoy SC-121, battered but still in formation, sailed into harbor on March 15, 1943; the supply lines to Great Britain remained open.

The British broke the new German naval radio cipher late in March, and once again the Allies were able to route the convoys around most of the wolf packs. More long-range aircraft, equipped with new radar sets, also became available, and although it was as yet only barely apparent the tide of the Atlantic war was about to turn in the Allies' favor. Driven from the surface, the U-boats were forced to make more attacks submerged, where their slow underwater speed and limited endurance meant that they could not keep up with the convoys or quickly escape an attacking escort. The wolf-pack tactics began to falter.

Escort Group A-3 persevered through March 1943 and escorted Convoy ON-175 westward across the Atlantic, arriving unscathed in Newfoundland on April 7. The CGC *Duane* and the Canadian destroyer HMCS *Skeena* reinforced the group, and they departed for Great Britain again on April 11, escorting Convoy HX-233.

Convoy HX-233: success
For five days no U-boat made contact, but on April 16 the U-262 (KL Heintz Francke) sighted the convoy. The *Spencer* picked the U-boat up on radar and attacked, forcing it to submerge. While the cutter failed to destroy the sub, its prompt attack prevented Francke from sending a contact report. However, another U-boat also located the convoy and guided in two more.

One freighter was torpedoed, and after the *Spencer* screened the rescue of survivors its sonar operator located U-175 as it attempted a submerged daylight attack from within the convoy. The U-boat's commanding officer, Kapitänleutnant Heinrich Bruns, had the tanker SS *G. Harrison Smith* in his attack periscope when the *Spencer* intervened. Sailing between the columns of merchantmen, the cutter delivered three accurate attacks; as one of U-175's

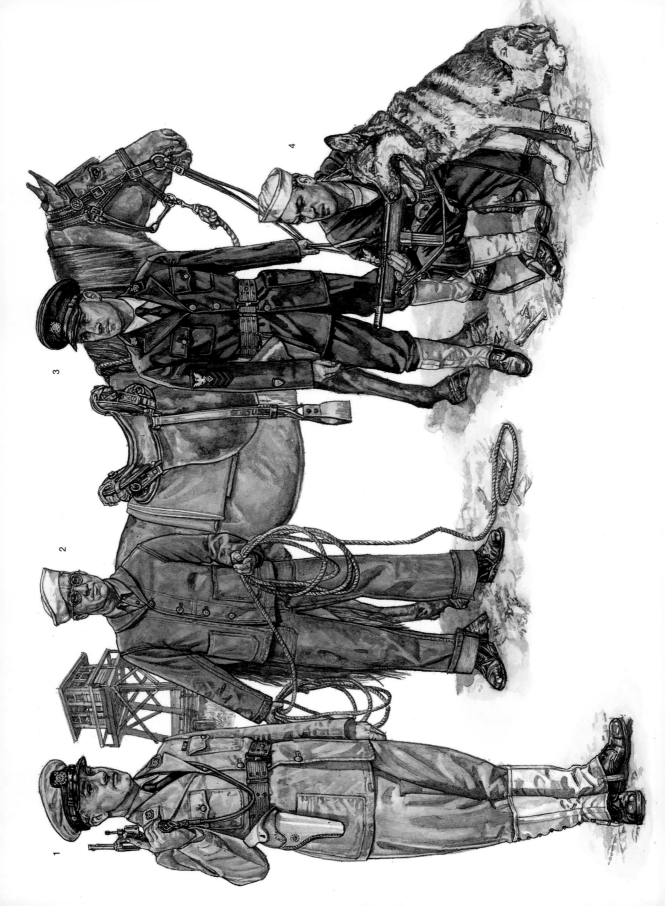

crew later recounted, "The [depth charges] were bad... everything was shaking... we came up and saw you in the periscope, but you saw us and we knew it was all over... our chance to get you was gone." The submarine surfaced, and the *Spencer*, *Duane*, and many of the naval gun crews posted aboard the merchant ships opened fire. The U-175's captain ordered the dive valves opened and his crew abandoned ship. The *Spencer* sent over a boarding party, but when Lt Ross P. Bullard and Boatswain's Mate C.S. "Mike" Hall climbed aboard it was clear that the U-boat was sinking too fast to salvage. (Nevertheless, Bullard had the distinction of becoming the first American serviceman to board an enemy warship "underway at sea" since the early 19th century.) Thanks to a calm sea and good visibility the USCG cutters rescued all 41 surviving German seamen.

ANTISUBMARINE OPERATIONS FROM MAY 1943

Although the crews did not realize it at the time, the Battle of the Atlantic had finally reached a tipping-point. "Ultra" intelligence, the closing at last of the "air gap" with the aid of long-range B-24 Liberator bombers, radar, "huff duff," growing Allied numbers and increasingly aggressive and confident escort tactics combined to achieve a clear victory over the U-boats during May 1943. That month the Allies sank 41 of Doenitz's boats, and on the 24th the admiral, realizing that the battle had turned against him, informed Hitler that he was withdrawing his submarines from the vital northern convoy routes. The Coast Guard's Secretary-class cutters were transferred to the central Atlantic, Mediterranean, and Caribbean convoy lanes. Although the retreat of the U-boats from the North Atlantic marked a strategic victory for the Allies, Doenitz continued to send his captains into the Atlantic in piecemeal fashion until the end of the war. Critical Allied resources were therefore still needed to construct escort vessels, and two such classes of warships, the mass-produced destroyer escorts and frigates, began to enter Coast Guard service in 1943.

The Coast Guard ultimately manned 30 destroyer escorts, formed into five escort divisions of six destroyers each, each division under the command of a

---

C

THE HOME FRONT, 1941–45
1: MEMBER, USCG AUXILIARY, SUMMER KHAKIS
2: MEMBER, USCG AUXILIARY, WORK UNIFORM
3: USCG RESERVIST (TEMPORARY) PETTY OFFICER 1st CLASS, MOUNTED BEACH PATROL
4: USCG PETTY OFFICER 3rd CLASS, DOG PATROL

The uniforms adopted for the part-time civilian volunteer personnel of the Coast Guard Auxiliary and the Coast Guard Reserves (Temporary) land establishment were similar to those used by the Surfmen, consisting of a single-breasted blue tunic and visored cap with appropriate "seal" insignia (see Plate H3), and **(C1)** a khaki version for warmer climates. In most cases the Auxiliarists wore a simpler version of the clothing worn by the USCG and USCGR (T), a khaki shirt and trousers and brown leather boat shoes. While working on vessels Auxiliarists wore denim workclothes **(C2)**. The most interesting uniform was that worn by members of the Coast Guard mounted beach patrols **(C3)**, with riding breeches and leather or canvas web leggings. Those assigned to security details or beach patrols were issued basic sidearms such as the Smith & Wesson .38cal revolver. Other small-arms used by Coast Guard patrols were the M1911A1 semiautomatic pistol (.45cal ACP), .30cal M1903 Springfield rifle, 12-gauge shotguns (Winchester M1897 and other makes), Thompson submachine gun (Models 1921, 1928A1, M1, & M1A1), and also the Model 50 Reising – also in .45cal ACP – as illustrated here **(C4)**. This handler's German Shepherd has a set of the new canvas boots, designed to protect the CG Dog Patrol animals from sustaining cut feet from oyster shells during the long treks along the nation's beaches on antisaboteur patrol. See Plates H9 & H11 for details of beach patrol and port security rating patches. In the background is one of the many beach watchtowers erected along American coasts.

A good comparison between the khaki uniforms of a US Navy captain (left) and Coast Guard Cdr Harold Berdine, skipper of the cutter *Spencer*. They vary only in the officers' cap emblems, and in those "inboard" of the rank stripes on the shoulder boards – a five-point star for the Navy line officer, and the USCG shield for Berdine. The *Spencer* epitomized the breadth of the Coast Guard's contribution to the war at sea; two years after hunting U-boats in the Atlantic she would see action as an amphibious landing control ship in Manila Bay. (AdeQHA)

senior Coast Guard officer. After their crews were trained and their new warships had completed their shakedown exercises, they began escorting convoys to Great Britain and the Mediterranean. One became the first destroyer escort sunk by enemy action when U-255 (Olt Erich Harms) torpedoed the USS *Leopold* in the cold waters south of Iceland in March 1944. A sister ship, the USS *Joyce*, under the command of Coast Guard LtCdr Robert Wilcox, dodged two other torpedoes fired from the U-boat. He called out to the *Leopold*'s survivors, "We're dodging torpedoes – God bless you – we'll be back." The *Joyce* was unable to locate the elusive U-255; when Wilcox returned his crew rescued just 28 survivors from the *Leopold*, but the torpedo explosion and the icy waters had claimed the rest.

In April 1944 the *Joyce* avenged them. The tanker *Pan Pennsylvania* was torpedoed by U-550 (KL Klaus Hänert) as it straggled behind its eastward-bound convoy. The *Joyce* and the USS *Peterson* picked up survivors, and then the *Joyce* detected the U-boat on sonar as the Germans attempted to escape after hiding from the "pings" actually beneath the hull of the sinking tanker. The U-550's engineering officer later said: "We waited for your ship to leave; soon we could hear nothing, so we thought the escort vessels had gone; but as soon as we started to move – bang!" The *Joyce* delivered a depth-charge pattern that bracketed the submerged submarine, and survivors reported that one actually bounced off the boat's casing before it exploded. Forced to the surface, U-550's crew manned their deck guns and opened fire. The *Joyce*, *Peterson*, and a Navy destroyer escort, the USS *Gandy*, all returned fire; the *Gandy* rammed the U-boat, and the *Peterson* dropped two shallow-set depth charges which exploded near the hull. Hänert's crew prepared scuttling charges and abandoned ship; the *Joyce* rescued 13 of the U-boat men, one of whom later died from wounds received during the battle. A mere 13 minutes had passed from the moment when the *Joyce* detected U-550 to the moment it surrendered – a striking demonstration of the effectiveness of Allied antisubmarine capabilities. Although all three warships shared credit for the kill, it was the *Joyce*'s depth-charge attack that brought the U-boat to the surface and ensured its destruction.

The increased Allied naval strength allowed the formation of free-ranging hunter-killer groups as well as close escorts for the convoys; with the sole task of hunting down and destroying U-boats, these groups accumulated a growing tally of successes. One such group consisted of the Coast Guard-manned *Pride*, *Menges*, *Mosely*, and *Lowe*, and was commanded by Cdr Reginald French. On March 18, 1945 they tracked and located U-866 (Olt Peter Rogowsky) after it was reported operating off the coast of Nova Scotia. The *Lowe* made two depth-charge runs and the *Menges* another; soon wreckage floated to the

The turning of the tide in the Battle of the Atlantic from May 1943 also saw the Coast Guard beginning to receive larger destroyer escorts; eventually the USCG would man 30 of these, in five escort divisions each commanded by a Coast Guard officer. One destroyer, the USS *Leopold*, was torpedoed and lost with nearly all her crew in March 1944. (AdeQHA)

surface, confirming the loss of U-866 with all hands. In late March 1945 the U-857 (KL Rudolf Premauer), which had also made the now nearly suicidal crossing of the Atlantic into North American waters, torpedoed an empty tanker. A hunter-killer group under the command of the *Pride*'s former skipper, Cdr Ralph R.Curry – who now flew his flag from the frigate *Knoxville* – was ordered to find and sink the U-boat. Curry knew his business by now; late in February his division had tracked down and sunk the U-869 (KL Helmut Neuerburg) off Morocco. On the morning of April 7, Curry's sonar operator located the U-857 hiding on the ocean floor off Cape Cod, and the boat was duly destroyed.

On May 4, 1945, Admiral Doenitz – named as the new Führer in Hitler's will when he committed suicide late in April – ordered his U-boats to surrender to the Allies. However, the commander of U-853, who was then patrolling off Rhode Island, either did not receive the order or chose to ignore it, and the sub torpedoed the steamer SS *Black Point* on May 5. The frigate USS *Moberly*, in concert with the USS *Atherton*, located and sank U-853 in a coordinated attack that finally brought the Battle of the Atlantic to a close. The Coast Guard's final military action in the North Atlantic occurred later in May, when the cutters *Durant* and *Vance* accepted the surrender of U-873, and U-234 surrendered to the USS *Forsyth*.

D: BY SEA, AIR AND LAND, 1942–45

1: USCG LIEUTENANT IN KHAKIS, CARIBBEAN
A wide variety of uniforms were employed by the Coast Guard in performance of their multi-faceted duties. This lieutenant's khaki shirt and trousers were standard wear for those in warm or tropical climates, with rank bars pinned to the collar points. Note that his "battleship gray"-painted M1 helmet has the distinctive USCG officer's eagle and anchor stenciled on the front above rank bars. Patrol duty in Caribbean waters was far from a vacation; when the U-boats first moved south in summer 1942 they enjoyed almost unopposed conditions, and were often able to use their heavy deck guns in daylight surface actions.

2: USCG LIEUTENANT PILOT, IN "AVIATION GREENS"
This floatplane pilot wears the US Navy aviator officer's distinctive forest-green kersey uniform – an echo of the Marine greens adopted by World War I Navy aviators in place of their impractical whites. The jacket had four pockets with buttoned three-point flaps, a bi-swing back and integral belt, three brown/bronze USCG front buttons, and black sleeve insignia. Both green-topped visored caps and green garrison caps might be worn with the uniform, with appropriate emblems. Note the gold Navy pilot's wings on his left breast. Naval regulations specified that "wearing of the aviation green uniform when that uniform is designated as the uniform of the day is mandatory only for commissioned and warrant officers designated naval aviators, and CPOs designated naval aviation pilots, serving in pilot status."

3: USCG CHIEF PETTY OFFICER PILOT, IN "GRAYS"
CPOs wore a blue officer-style uniform with a visored cap and an eight-button reefer jacket, but enlisted-style combined rank-and-rating sleeve patches. On whites and khakis these insignia were worn in black; on the blues the eagle and rating symbol were white, the latter enclosed by a single top "rocker" and three chevrons in scarlet. Men who achieved 12 years' service with good conduct wore silver eagles and gold rockers and chevrons, and three gold diagonal service stripes. This CPO wears the gray uniform, of the same style as the khakis, that was introduced as an officer's working-dress alternative to both whites and khakis by an order of April 16, 1943; the grays were extended to chief petty officers from June 3 that year (and from March 31, 1944, to cooks and stewards). During World War II the Coast Guard, like the Navy, ran short of pilots, and began to train enlisted men as well as officers. This CPO's rank and rating is worn in black on his left sleeve, above the two service stripes indicating between eight and 12 years' service. As an enlisted man he would display the black USCG shield on his right forearm only. His aviator wings are in silver instead of officer's gold; for detail of his cap emblem, see Plate H1.

4: USCG PETTY OFFICER 2nd CLASS; UNIT 26, COAST GUARD CONSTRUCTION DETACHMENT
This seaman from a Coast Guard Construction Detachment has been issued the olive-drab herringbone twill fatigue uniform commonly worn in the United States Marine Corps, and brown field shoes (he would also wear round Navy/Marine-type "dog tags"). His 2nd Class rating patch with the emblem of the Electrical Branch is worn on his right sleeve. Coast Guard personnel serving on shore usually had their M1 "steel pots" painted in olive drab in contrast to the "battleship gray" normally worn by shipboard personnel.

The Coast Guard's contribution to Allied victory over the U-boats went far beyond what had originally been expected of them. Although the majority of the Coast Guard units could not claim a U-boat "kill," this was not the only measure of success. Each escort helped to keep the U-boats at bay, ultimately ensuring the timely and safe arrival in Europe and North Africa of the cargoes and personnel that ensured victory in the land war. Coast Guard units also rescued nearly 1,000 Allied and Axis survivors along the North Atlantic convoy routes, 1,600 along the American coast, and 200 in the Mediterranean, thereby fulfilling the service's most historic mission.

The Coast Guard looks back with pride to this legacy, which earned the respect and admiration of both allies and enemies when their paths crossed with America's oldest sea service. One former crewman of U-175 was overheard by intelligence officers telling a fellow prisoner-of-war: "When I came up on deck, I saw one of those cutters... making straight for us. It was... Coast Guard! Do you know them, those American ones?"

THE MEDITERRANEAN AND EUROPEAN THEATERS

Besides duty in the North Atlantic and along America's shores, Coast Guard warships escorted convoys across the central Atlantic and into the Mediterranean. Although the seas were calmer they were still subject to attack from U-boats and, once past Gibraltar and into the Mediterranean, from German aircraft that proved to be just as deadly as the submarines.

On one voyage in April 1944 the Pearl Harbor veteran CGC *Taney* served as the flagship for the two accompanying escort divisions, one of which was entirely Coast Guard-manned. Guarding an Africa-bound convoy from the United States, they found the trip uneventful until they entered the Mediterranean. Even at this relatively late stage in the war Luftwaffe units based in Italy and southern France could still prove formidable, and when the convoy was off the coast of Algeria at least 20 German torpedo-bombers attacked under cover of dusk. One torpedo obliterated the ammunition-laden freighter *Paul Hamilton*, killing all aboard. Three more merchant ships were seriously damaged, and another torpedo blew apart the destroyer USS *Lansdale*. The Coast Guard-manned USS *Menges*, commanded by LtCdr Frank M. McCabe, survived the attacks, downed one of the bombers with antiaircraft fire, and rescued 137 *Lansdale* survivors as well as two German airmen.

After delivering the surviving merchantmen to Tunisia the warships turned around to escort another convoy back to the United States. While they were still off the Algerian coast, Oberleutnant Horst-Arno Fenski surfaced his U-371 behind the convoy, and the *Menges* picked it up on radar. McCabe immediately reversed course to investigate, but before submerging U-371 fired an acoustic torpedo at the closing destroyer, blowing the stern off the *Menges* and killing 31 crewmen. Although seriously damaged she remained afloat, and McCabe and his crew stayed with their ship while the Coast Guard-manned USS *Pride* (Cdr Ralph R. Curry) located the submerged U-boat and seriously damaged it with a depth-charge attack. The *Pride* continued to track the submarine and, in concert with an international team of escorts, cornered it near the African coast. Surrounded, with water leaking into the hull and the batteries almost dead, the U-boat surfaced; her crew scuttled her and abandoned ship, being picked up by the Allied warships.

The *Menges* was towed safely into port, and later back to the United States, where she received a new stern cannibalized from another damaged destroyer escort. The USS *Menges* rejoined the fleet and, after making two more convoy-escort runs, reported for duty under Cdr French in the first Coast Guard-manned hunter-killer group to see service in the North Atlantic (see above).

THE NORMANDY LANDINGS

The US Coast Guard was an integral part of Operation *Neptune*, the codename given to the amphibious assault and naval support operations for Operation *Overlord*. These operations were divided between two task forces that would gather the troops up from ports all over southern Britain and land them on the beaches of Normandy, give them gunfire support, and keep them supplied. The Western Naval Task Force, under the command of US Navy

The cost: this Coast Guardsman died at his battle station aboard the USS *Menges*, one of 31 of her crew to die when she was torpedoed by U-371 in the Mediterranean in April 1944. He represents the old Coast Guard expression: "You have to go out, but you don't have to come back." (AdeQHA)

Troops paddle ashore in small boats from a Coast Guard-manned Landing Craft, Infantry (Large). Under combat conditions these shallow-draft craft glided right in to the beach, lowering gangways each side of the bow to allow a full rifle company to disembark; since this took three or four minutes, the LCI(L) was normally employed to carry follow-on waves rather than the initial assault troops. Not an ocean-going craft, it was used for relatively short-range shore-to-shore operations, first entering battle in the Mediterranean in July 1943 and seeing extensive use in the Sicily and Salerno landings. (AdeQHA)

Rear Admiral Alan Kirk, transported the US First Army to the American assault areas codenamed "Utah" and "Omaha." The Eastern Naval Task Force, commanded by Royal Navy Rear Admiral Sir Philip Vian, landed the British Second Army on assault areas to the east of the American landings, codenamed "Gold," "Juno" and "Sword."

The Coast Guard presence centered on Assault Group O-1, which landed troops of the 1st Infantry Division – the "Big Red One" – on the easternmost beaches of the "Omaha" assault area. Commanded by Coast Guard Capt Edward H. Fritzsche, this assault group consisted of the *Samuel Chase*, the US Navy's USS *Henrico* and the Royal Navy's HMS *Empire Anvil*; six Landing Craft, Infantry, Large – LCI(L)s; six Landing Ships, Tank – LSTs; and 97 smaller craft. Coast Guard Capt Miles Imlay doubled as the deputy assault commander of Assault Group O-1 and as commander of its Coast Guard-manned LCI(L) Flotilla 10. The battle-tested landing craft of Flotilla 10 were divided between the "Omaha" and "Utah" landing forces and were the heart of the Coast Guard's contribution to the invasion. Flotilla Ten consisted of a total of 36 LCI(L)s, of which 24 were manned by the Coast Guard and were veterans of the landings on Sicily and at Salerno. These small vessels could carry 200 assault troops and land them directly on a beach via two gangways deployed on either side of the vessel's bow.

Assault Group O-1 was the largest Coast Guard command in Operation *Neptune* but was not the only one. Further west, US Navy Rear Admiral Don P. Moon commanded the assault on the "Utah" beaches from the force flagship, the Coast Guard-manned attack transport USS *Bayfield*. The *Bayfield*, commanded by Coast Guard Capt Lyndon Spencer, served as the nerve center for the entire "Utah" assault. Among the other vessels that landed the 4th "Ivyleaf" Infantry Division at "Utah" were the Coast Guard-manned USS *Joseph T. Dickman*, and the USS *Barnett* with a partial Coast Guard crew, alongside the HMS *Empire Gauntlet*. The Coast Guard also participated in the British and Canadian landings; four CG-manned LSTs trained with and carried troops and equipment for the landings at "Gold," "Juno" and "Sword." The Coast Guard also partially manned many other US Navy vessels, including the transport USS *Charles Carroll*.

Beyond contributing leadership and men to crew US Navy vessels, the Coast Guard also provided the Allied fleet with cutters of its own. In the weeks prior to the landings President Roosevelt had suggested that Operation *Neptune* needed a rescue flotilla. Since naval resources were stretched to the limit, Adm Ernest J. King (C-in-C US Fleet and Chief of Naval Operations) looked to the Coast Guard. The service was operating 83ft patrol boats, nicknamed the "Matchbox Fleet," on antisubmarine duty along the east coast of the United States; although they were constructed of wood and had gasoline engines, they were available. Admiral King ordered 60 of these craft shipped to England as cargo; renamed Rescue Flotilla 1 for the invasion, they were commanded by Coast Guard Reserve Cdr Alexander Stewart, with hull numbers assigned sequentially from 1 to 60 for identification. SHAEF planners ordered half of the patrol boats to sail in support of the Eastern Naval Task Force while the other half sailed with Kirk's western command.

In preparation for Normandy, USN Rear Adm John L. Hall, commander of the "Omaha" assault force, supervised the training of all Navy and Coast Guard personnel. Hall established joint amphibious schools where landing-craft crews were trained in small-boat handling, ship-to-shore movement, and beach landings and extractions; they were also instructed in beach-party operations, beach markings, salvage and general maintenance. Coast Guardsmen trained together in joint exercises with the Army assault troops. They practiced small-scale landings along the British coast and made five full-scale practice assaults at Slapton Sands in Devon, whose beaches were similar to those of Normandy.

Coast Guard landing-craft crewmen assisting a casualty off an invasion beach in 1944. (Some Coast Guardsmen who served with landing craft were authorized to wear the American Naval Amphibious Forces left shoulder insignia. This patch, embroidered in golden-yellow on a scarlet tombstone-shaped background, copied the design of the British Combined Operations forces patch.) Of particular interest is the Coast Guard war correspondent (right), identified by his helmet stencil "USCG/CORRESPONDENT". He wears what appears to be a modified or custom-made Parsons-type field jacket, and an uninflated life belt of the type issued to the Normandy assault troops, and is armed with a Colt M1911A1 pistol and a knife – see Plate E3. (AdeQHA)

A wartime image showing the standard USCG walking-out uniform of a petty officer second class. Note the white USCG shield worn on the right forearm only by enlisted men; this was the only thing that immediately distinguished the "coastie" from the Navy "gob." The Coast Guard used the same system of rank and rating patches as the Navy. Almost every man trained and qualified in a trade ("rating") was a petty officer of first, second or third class, and on the blue uniform wore the white eagle above the white emblem of his rating, above one, two, or three scarlet chevrons. His rank would be formally expressed as e.g. "Signalman 2nd Class", marked in that case by the "crow" above crossed semaphore flags, above two red chevrons. The combined patch was worn on his right sleeve if he served in the Seaman branch, i.e. notionally on deck or turret duties, while all others wore theirs on their left sleeve (as did aviation ratings). (AdeQHA)

Imlay's Flotilla 10 participated in many of these exercises, as did most of the Coast Guard-manned LSTs and transports. The intense training, combined with the experience gained during the invasions in the Mediterranean, was critical to ensuring a successful landing of troops and supplies on the beaches.

The invasion beaches

The Normandy invasion was to take place in the Bay of the Seine on the south coast of the English Channel, between the Cotentin Peninsula and the port of Le Havre. Some 55 miles broad and 20 deep, its waters were shallow and had a considerable tidal range (but when the wind blew from the north they could be very choppy). The planned landing beaches covered about 45 miles of the bay's shoreline. Westernmost was the "Utah" area, stretching 8 miles southward along the low-lying southeastern coast of the Cotentin Peninsula. Directly to the east was "Omaha," covering 12 miles of generally hilly terrain. United States forces were assigned to take both of these areas, with important assistance from the navies of Great Britain and other Allies. British and Canadian troops would assault the areas codenamed "Gold" (British), "Juno" (Canadian), and "Sword" (British), which ran 20 miles eastward from Omaha. This sector ended at the mouth of the Orne River, some 15 miles west of Le Havre, where the German Navy had based a group of potentially very dangerous torpedo boats.

Amongst the thousands of ships making the voyage from England to the coast of France would be 97 warships, transports, landing vessels, and cutters manned by Coast Guard crews. When the D-Day invasion actually commenced in the early hours of June 6, 1944, Coast Guard coxswains and boat crews would land combat forces on the beach under heavy enemy fire, while Coast Guard officers directed the landings on the most fiercely contested areas of "Omaha" beach. Coast Guard cutters and their crews would rescue survivors of sunken landing craft from the cold waters of the English Channel, while other Coast Guardsmen helped assemble and maintain the huge prefabricated artificial "Mulberry harbors." Devised by the British to be towed across the Channel and installed off the American and British beaches, these were capable of handling 12,000 tons of supplies per day. In late June a Coast Guard-led assault force would help liberate the vitally important port city of Cherbourg.

The landings

The landing vessels of the "Utah" assault force passed the warships of the gunfire support squadron at their station 11,000 yards off the landing area, which opened fire on German gun emplacements at 5.30am on June 6. The landing area was a gently sloping beach backed by sand dunes, divided into two sections codenamed Beach Red and Beach Green. The German defenses here included 28 heavy batteries of fixed artillery of up to 21cm caliber and a large number of mobile 8.8cm guns. Two US Navy control vessels guided the landing craft, and a number of amphibious tanks, in from an assembly point miles off shore to their respective beaches. Despite the meticulous forward planning, confusion reigned on the beaches throughout the day. Beach Red's control ship struck a mine and sank, and the featureless nature of the beaches, further obscured by naval gunfire and rocket explosions, all combined to confuse the remaining control vessels and landing craft. Fortunately the mistaken landfalls on "Utah" turned out to be, if anything, advantageous. When the situation had stabilized Capt Fritzche turned command of Assault Group 0-1 over to Capt Imlay, and returned to Great Britain.

Captain Imlay was assigned as the port director for the Omaha "Mulberry," which was soon handling as much traffic as some of the world's larger ports. These prefabricated wharves, protected by blockship breakwaters codenamed "Gooseberries," allowed men, tanks, and heavy equipment to be landed from landing craft and ships and to drive directly to the beaches to augment and supply the five Allied divisions put ashore in Normandy on D-Day. The Coast Guard-manned *Bayfield* continued to operate as the command ship for "Utah" for 19 days after D-Day, throughout which time her surgeons remained busy caring for the wounded. The other transports and Coast Guard-manned landing craft continued to bring reinforcements and supplies to France and to return to England with wounded and prisoners; one, LST-261, made no fewer than 53 crossings in the days following D-Day. LCI (Landing Craft Infantry) numbers 85, 91, 92, and 93 were lost in the Normandy landings; 18 Coast Guardsmen paid the ultimate price on D-Day itself, and 38 more were seriously wounded, mainly while crewing the LCIs. There were more casualties to come that summer from mines, torpedoes, and air attacks as the ships plied the Channel between England and France.

During Operation *Neptune/Overlord* the Coast Guardsmen also carried out their time-honored task of saving lives, albeit under enemy fire on a shoreline thousands of miles from home. Rescue Flotilla 1 saved more than 400 men on D-Day alone, and by the time the unit was decommissioned in December 1944 they had saved 1,438 souls. Today a small memorial to the "Matchbox Fleet" stands at the harborside in Poole, Dorset, as one of the few tangible reminders of the Coast Guard's role in the Normandy landings. The inscription reads:

From this quay, 60 cutters of the United States Coast Guard Rescue Flotilla 1 departed for the Normandy Invasion, 6 June 1944. These 83ft boats, built entirely of wood, and the 840 crew members were credited with saving the lives of 1,437 men and 1 woman. In remembrance of the service of Rescue Flotilla 1, and with appreciation of the kindnesses of the people of Poole to the crews, this plaque is given by the men and women of the United States Coast Guard.

A seaman of the US Coast Guard wearing the flat-top cap commonly referred to as the "Donald Duck"; this was regulation headgear in the European theater for both Navy and Coast Guard enlisted men. (AdeQHA)

THE PACIFIC THEATER

THE ALEUTIANS

When war broke out in Europe in September 1939 the Coast Guard already had the nucleus of an organization operating in Alaska. When planning the Territory's defense the Army and Navy relied upon their experience, since the Coast Guard had been the earliest government agency operating in Alaska. Coast Guard officials were among the first to plead for an extension of transportation facilities, which were notably poor; for improvement of harbors and navigational aids, and for general defense needs.

When the United States entered World War II in December 1941 there were fewer than 17,000 troops in Alaska. In 1942 Canada and the United States, under a mutual defense agreement, constructed a network of bases in the southeastern "panhandle," and others along the southern coast and the Alaskan Peninsula. The Navy extended its chief base at Dutch Harbor in the Aleutian Islands chain, set up air and submarine bases at Kodiak and Sitka, and established radio stations throughout Alaska. The USCG's surface craft, aircraft, and personnel played appropriate parts in the military operations preceding and during the Aleutians campaign.

As a diversionary move in conjunction with their strike against Midway, in June 1942 the Japanese bombed Dutch Harbor and landed troops on Kiska and Attu islands. Here they remained, primarily in a defensive posture, to prevent any westward movement by American forces towards Japan through the Aleutians. In late September 1942 the bulk of the Japanese garrison at Attu was transferred to Kiska, leaving Attu barely defended, but since it was distant from friendly bases the Americans did not attempt to reclaim the island. However, on October 29, 1942 some 500 Japanese troops returned, establishing a base at Holtz Bay under the command of LtCol Hiroshi Yanekawa. The size and strength of the Attu garrison grew steadily over the next few months to about 2,300 men, but after an action off the Komandorski Islands in March 1943 the Japanese ceased attempts to supply Attu and Kiska by surface vessels, and thereafter stores trickled in by submarine only. During the winter of 1942/43 Kiska was also reinforced by sea, raising the garrison to some 5,200 Japanese by the following July.

During May 11–30, 1943, US forces landed on and recaptured Attu, though hampered by foggy weather, sodden terrain and a costly resistance (only 26 Japanese allowed themselves to be captured alive). In July the US Navy increased their bombardment of Kiska, delivering 2,793 shells on 22 July in conjunction with ongoing aerial attacks. After the tough fighting on Attu the

E SEA DUTY, 1942–44

1: USCG SEAMAN; FOUL-WEATHER GEAR, NORTH ATLANTIC

A wartime instruction for seamen stated that "There are three layers of clothing involved in protecting yourself from winter cold. These are the underwear layer, the insulation layer, and the wind-and-water-resistant layer." The seaman illustrated here is wearing a fur-lined N-1 parka over his bib-fronted padded coveralls – both in shades of olive drab - and black cloth-and-rubber overboots with metal clips; he would normally wear a knitted wool cap under his hood. Such heavy clothing was essential for deck watches in winter, but would drag him down if he were unlucky enough to go overboard. In the winter seas its notional warmth would not save him from lapsing into unconsciousness after a few minutes, quickly followed by death from hypothermia or drowning.

2: USCG GUNNER'S MATE; TEMPERATE CLIMATE DECK CLOTHING, CONVOY ESCORT, NORTH ATLANTIC

This member of a 3in gun crew is wearing the second-pattern dark blue Navy deck jacket with knit collar, cuffs and waistband, but now with galoshes-style metal clips replacing the front zip fastener of the first pattern. His M1 helmet is painted "battleship gray," and he wears standard-issue Navy working dress of chambray shirt and denims.

3: USCG WAR CORRESPONDENT, NORMANDY LANDINGS

This Coast Guard-authorized war correspondent, from a photo published on page 39, displays his status by a "USCG/Correspondent" stencil on the front of the helmet, and by a patch on his left shoulder (his facial hair also marks him out as a civilian). His jacket appears to be a customized item based on the "M1941" or Parsons field jacket, with an external breast pocket; it is worn over HBT fatigue trousers and brown field shoes. The uninflated life belt around his waist obscures some of the items hooked to his web pistol belt, but the M1911A1 pistol and a US Navy Mk I fighting knife (manufactured by Camillus, Ka-Bar, and other firms) are identifiable.

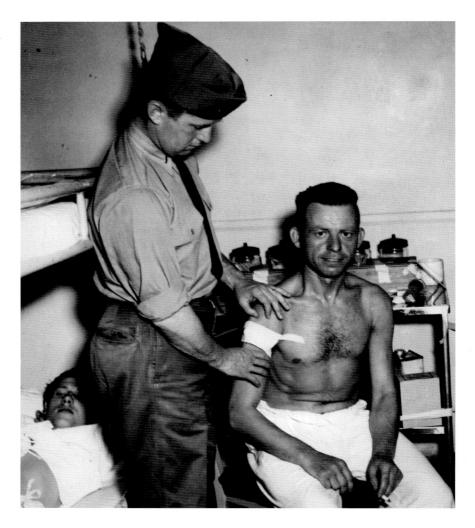

The US Public Health Service provided medical personnel for Coast Guard vessels; they wore the same uniforms and were distinguished only by their insignia. Here a PHS doctor aboard a Coast Guard-manned transport ship is dressing the injury of a German prisoner captured in Normandy. (AdeQHA)

American planners deployed a much larger force for the Kiska operation. About 29,000 Americans and 5,300 Canadian troops landed on the island on August 15 and 16 respectively, supported by a powerful fleet centered on three battleships and a heavy cruiser, supported by 168 aircraft. They found the island deserted; taking advantage of heavy fog more than two weeks previously, the Japanese had successfully evacuated Kiska without detection on 28 July (though leaving behind booby traps that killed upwards of 20 men as they secured the island).

The Coast Guard participated with the US Army and Navy and Canadian forces throughout the Aleutians campaign. On June 3, 1942, when Japanese aircraft attacked Dutch Harbor, the AA gunners on the cutter CGC *Onandaga* – one of the eight vessels in port – fired nearly 2,000 rounds, and several Japanese aircraft were shot down during the raid. The cutter *Nemeha* rescued the pilot of a downed Navy PBY patrol plane that was shot down by a Japanese Zero. The following month the combined efforts of a Canadian patrol aircraft, a Navy-commandeered fishing vessel, and the CGC *McLane* culminated in the sinking of Japanese submarine RO-61. In the campaign to regain the Aleutians, Coast Guard personnel manned troop transports such as the USS *Arthur Middleton* as well as small landing craft.

During the rest of the war the Coast Guard provided unglamorous but necessary services to support military operations in Alaska and the northern Pacific. They operated Navy post offices on most floating units and stations in Alaska. They maintained the Army's How beacon on Saint Paul Island, and operated radio surveillance stations at Ketchikan and Seward; built and operated an ANRAC station at Massacre Bay on Adak; and constructed, supported, and operated radio direction-finder stations. Between April 1943 and March 1944 a 140-man Coast Guard construction battalion built and placed into operation eight LORAN (Longe Range Navigation) stations in the western Aleutians and the Bering Sea, which were used extensively to guide bombers toward targets on the northern Japanese islands. The Coast Guard also provided diving services for vessel repair and salvage, ice-breaking patrols, fire-fighting boats for small coastal communities, and weather-reporting services to CAA stations in Alaska, and maintained a library of hydrographic information about Alaskan waters. They provided shore protection for all naval installations in southeast Alaska; built and maintained emergency anchorages for seaplanes and convoys; and planned and started construction of five new lighthouses. They also assisted in the Army's Alaska Spruce Program, and transported military personnel both on orders and on leave within Alaska, and touring United Service Organizations (USOs) entertainers throughout the Alaskan Territory.

PACIFIC AMPHIBIOUS OPERATIONS

The Solomons

On August 7, 1942, the armed forces of the United States embarked on their first major amphibious landings of the Pacific War. After the victories in the naval battles of the Coral Sea and Midway the Americans decided to counter Japanese advances in the Solomon Islands, which form two parallel lines that run northwest/southeast approximately 600 miles east of New Guinea. Tulagi and Guadalcanal, both at the southern end of the chain, were picked for an assault; Guadalcanal was strategically important because the Japanese were building an airfield there. Guadalcanal saw the Coast Guard's first major participation in the Pacific theater of operations; Coast Guardsmen played a significant role in the landings on that island, and thereafter they would be employed in every major amphibious operation throughout World War II, manning more than 350 ships and many hundreds more amphibious assault craft (Higgins boats, LCVPs, LCMs, and LVTs).[2]

For Guadalcanal, 18 of the 22 naval troop-carrying ships attached to the task force carried Coast Guard personnel. These men were assigned a central part in the landings – the operation of the landing craft; many of the Coast Guard coxswains had come from Life-Saving stations, and their experience with small boats made them seasoned boat-handlers. The initial landings on Guadalcanal in August 1942 opened a hard-fought campaign on that island lasting for nearly six months. Seven weeks after the initial landings, during an engagement near Point Cruz, Signalman 1st Class Douglas A. Munro died while rescuing a group of US Marines, and was posthumously awarded the World War II Coast Guard's only Congressional Medal of Honor.

2 For details of types of amphibious assault craft, the transport ships that supported landings, and how all were employed, see Elite 117: *US World War II Amphibious Tactics, Pacific Theater*, and Elite 144: *US World War II Amphibious Tactics, Mediterranean & European Theaters*.

The Coast Guard continued its supporting role as the Allies moved north and west. When, in June and July 1943, the Army and Marines made landings at several points on Rendova, New Georgia, and Vangunu islands, five transports with partial Coast Guard crews participated in the month-long operation. Approximately 40 miles from New Georgia, and located beyond the fortified and well-garrisoned island of Kolombangara, Vella Lavella was the next link in the chain of Japanese-held islands to be attacked. In a tactic repeated throughout the war, the Americans bypassed Kolombangara and landed Army troops on Vella Lavella on August 15; the partially CG-manned LST-334 and the fully manned LST-167 participated in the landings, and for weeks both assisted with the resupply of the force ashore. LST-167 was beached at Ruravai, Vella Lavella, on September 24 when three Japanese dive-bombers appeared just as the last piece of equipment rolled off the ship. After releasing their bombs the aircraft pulled out of their dive, where one burst into flames and another began trailing smoke under the continuous fire of AA guns from the landing ship. Two Japanese bombs struck the LST; both penetrated the main deck and exploded, one blowing a hole through the side of the hull and the other setting fire to 1,000 gallons of gasoline and 250 drums of oil on the tank deck. The intense fire forced most of the crew to abandon ship; two officers and eight men died in the attack, and another five were listed as missing. Vella Lavella was secured by American and Australian troops within the week; elsewhere, Coast Guardsmen were transporting other Aussie troops during the continuing campaign in New Guinea.[3]

The Gilberts and Marshalls

The Central Pacific campaign began with the capture of the Gilbert Islands chain, about 1,300 miles northeast of the Solomons. For the assaults on Tarawa and Makin atolls approximately 200 vessels were assembled, to put ashore 27,600 assault troops, 7,600 garrison troops, 6,000 vehicles, and 117,000 tons of cargo. The ships were organized into three main groups: the Assault Force, the Carrier Force, and the Defense Force. The Assault Force included many Coast Guard ships, and was further divided into a Northern Attack Force for Makin and a Southern Attack Force to land on Tarawa. These islands were taken during November 20–23, 1943, though at a heavy

3 See Elite 153: *The Australian Army in World War II.*

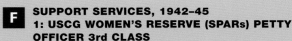

F

SUPPORT SERVICES, 1942–45
1: USCG WOMEN'S RESERVE (SPARs) PETTY OFFICER 3rd CLASS
Wartime recruiting pamphlets described the SPAR uniforms as "navy blue, semi-fitted garments." The blue service uniform consisted of a four-button blouse with rounded lapels and a six-gored skirt, of serge gabardine or tropical worsted. The Coast Guard shield was worn on the right sleeve, and the "seal" (see Plate H3) on the lapels. Rating badges and rank chevrons were worn on the sleeves. The SPARs had several "covers" depending on rank and order of dress – for enlisted women the basic headgear was this jaunty round-crowned, snap-brimmed hat with a "US COAST GUARD" hatband tally in gold letters. The SPARs had a variety of shirts, including work shirts, silk dress shirts and everyday pale blue cotton shirts.

2: SPARs ENSIGN
Women's Reserve officer uniforms differed slightly from that of the enlisted ranks. The gold USCG shield was worn on both sleeves above the gold rank rings, and the rings on their whites were bright blue – denoting Reserve ranks – instead of gold. The standard USCG officer's emblem is worn here on a white-covered SPARs officer's hat, often referred to as a "boat." However, no provision was made for women with the rank of commander or above to wear Reserve-blue "scrambled eggs" on the rolled brim. For informal use both officers and enlisted women wore garrison caps.

3: US NAVY CHAPLAIN
This chaplain assigned to the Coast Guard wears Navy officer's uniform with his distinctive insignia above his cuff rank rings.

A Coast Guardsman cradles a high explosive shell aboard the USS *Tacoma* in Dutch Harbor, Alaska, February 1945. The US Navy developed and used many different styles of clothing and cold weather gear during the war; winter "deck jackets" were probably the most cherished by serving sailors and are the most sought-after by collectors today. As seen here, most of those used in World War II evolved from a dark blue, waterproof, zip-front design that was very similar in appearance to the US Army's winter combat jacket ("tanker's jacket"). In 1943 a second version of this design featured an improved front closure with metal clips – see Plate E2. This seaman is posing for the photo wearing only the fiber liner of his M1 helmet – for "general quarters" the steel shell would of course be added. (AdeQHA)

cost in American lives; 2nd Marine Division had to virtually annihilate the dug-in Japanese garrison on Tarawa before the atoll was secured, and many painful lessons were learned about the conduct of contested landings.

The Coast Guard once again played an important role during the Marshall Islands campaign in February 1944, when the US forces focused their attention on Kwajalein, Majuro, and Eniwetok atolls. Operation *Flintlock* called for Majuro to be taken first to provide an anchorage for the fleet; Kwajalein would be assaulted from both ends the following day; and after some three months to consolidate, an assault force would then land on Eniwetok. A Joint Expeditionary Force comprising nearly 300 vessels and more than 84,000 men was assembled to take these atolls, split into a northern group for an attack on Roi and Namur islands within the widespread Kwajalein atoll, a southern group for an assault on Kwajalein island itself, and a third group to land on Majuro, which the Japanese had virtually evacuated the previous November. The Coast Guard-manned transport *Cambria* (APA-36) served as the flagship for the Majuro task force, which steamed into position to land troops on January 31; on February 1 the task force entered the lagoon uncontested, and this atoll would serve as the staging area for Central Pacific fleet operations for the next several months.

On January 30 the Northern Attack Force, including six transports with full or partial Coast Guard crews, gathered to strike at Roi and Namur islands. The following day the fire-support vessels and aircraft began subjecting the Japanese garrisons on those and other nearby islands to an intense bombardment that killed a large number of the islands' 3,700 defenders. Troops of 4th Marine Division landed on February 1 with almost no opposition, and all Japanese resistance on Roi and Namur ceased shortly after noon the next day. By February 7, with some mopping-up actions, the attack force secured about 55 islands and islets.

The Southern Attack Force arrived off Kwajalein on January 30, 1944, and the battleships and cruisers immediately began a devastating bombardment. The Coast Guard had four fully or partially manned transports active in this assault; the 7th Infantry Division's landings went so well that the Reserve Group – including five more transports with entire or partial Coast Guard crews – did not even participate, and Kwajalein and the nearby islands were secured by the afternoon of February 4. The quick capture of Majuro and Kwajalein encouraged the American commanders to greatly advance the date for the landings on Eniwetok, from May 10 to February 17, committing the unused Reserve Group and troops who had not been put ashore.

The barrier islands at Eniwetok atoll were attacked one at a time, each in turn being subjected to a heavy and continuous bombardment in preparation for the landings. The first island selected for capture was Engebi, and on February 18 the Coast Guard-manned troop transport *Heywood* (AP-12) and

attack transport *Arthur Middleton* (APA-25) participated in these landings, with one of the latter's boats leading the first wave to the beach. After the first waves of landing craft reached shore, the transports moved closer in to facilitate the unloading of men and supplies. Again, the bombardment had been so effective that the assault waves met only light resistance. On the 19th, while the Engebi landings proceeded, the transports prepared to land troops on Eniwetok, and by February 21 that island was secured. Parry Island was more strongly held than anticipated, however, and landings there were postponed until D-Day + 5 – February 22. After a four-day bombardment the assault troops quickly overcame the Japanese defenders, securing Parry Island in just 12 hours.

New Guinea and the Marianas

Far to the southwest, on the north coast of the huge and mountainous island of New Guinea, Australian successes on the Huon Peninsula by late April 1944 prompted Gen MacArthur to leapfrog troops 250 miles northwestwards to seize the Japanese base at Hollandia and push beyond it. At dawn on April 22, US troops landed on the shores of Humbolt Bay and Tanahmerah Bay with little or no opposition. The Coast Guard had 21 fully or partially manned LSTs, transports and frigates attached to the invasion forces; these landings completely surprised the Japanese, who were mainly driven into the chaotic jungle mountains of the interior, giving up harbors and airfields. On May 17, US and Australian warships bombarded Wakde Island, off the coast 115 miles west of Hollandia; by that evening the Allied landing forces had established an 8-mile beachhead, finally securing the island and its airfield on the evening of the 19th.

In the Central Pacific the next island objective was the Marianas group, lying some 1,300 miles east of the Philippines and about 1,300 miles due south of Tokyo. The invasion forces included a total of 535 ships carrying more than 127,000 troops in four and one-half reinforced divisions, to assault the most important islands at the southern end of the Marianas chain: Guam, Saipan, and Tinian (the lightly defended islands north of these had little

Official Coast Guard painting of Munro's last moments, while leading a flotilla of Higgins boats in to evacuate Marines from Point Cruz. (USCG Historian's Office)

strategic value). For this Operation *Forager* the Northern Attack Force that sailed for Saipan and Tinian consisted of 37 transports including the Coast Guard-manned *Callaway*, *Cambria*, *Arthur Middleton*, *Leonard Wood*, and LSTs 19, 23, 166 and 169; seven other transports had partial Coast Guard crews. The Southern Attack Force, steaming for Guam, included the Coast Guard-manned transports *Aquarius* and *Centaurus*, the cargo ships *Cor Caroli* and *Sterope*, LSTs 24, 70, 71, and 207, and seven other vessels with partial Coast Guard crews. The Reserve Force included the Coast Guard-manned *Cavalier*.

The transports assembled off Saipan while the fire-support ships and carrier aircraft began an intense bombardment at 8am on June 15, 1944. Some 8,000 men of 2nd and 4th Marine Divisions headed towards the beach along a 4-mile front in 600 LVTs ("amtracs"), supported by 150 howitzer-armed LVT(A)s. The LCIs and even the little LCVPs could not be used to land the initial assault waves because their deeper draft prevented them from crossing the reefs that fringed the island; these landing craft ferried Marines to the edge of the reefs, where they transferred into the shallower-draft LVTs, which then shuttled back and forth between the reefs and the beachhead with loads of troops – trips made hazardous by the fire of the Japanese defenders. As the battle raged it became imperative that larger craft be brought in to the beachhead.

The Coast Guard mission became critical that morning when the main assault on the port town of Charan-Kanoa bogged down while Marines clung to the beachhead with limited ammunition, medical supplies and support. Searching over a wide area of the lagoon, a Coast Guard landing craft, under intense enemy fire, probed until it found a 4ft-deep, 150ft-wide channel and marked a passage, allowing a steady stream of larger craft to carry supplies to the beach. The Marines eventually secured the beachhead and pushed the Japanese garrison further inland. The amphibious assault on Saipan was considered a model operation in every respect; about 20,000 Marines had landed on Saipan by 6pm that evening, completely overwhelming the initial defense. Even so, it took longer than anticipated to finally destroy isolated Japanese units, and it was 25 days before the island was securely in American hands. This, together with Japanese carrier movements, disrupted the original plan to begin landings on Guam on June 18.

Guam was the largest and the most important island in the Marianas group. Unlike Saipan and other islands that had been Japanese possessions since the end of World War I, this United States possession had been captured only on December 11, 1941, and it was not as heavily fortified; nevertheless, by 1944 it had a large garrison. Guam's large size made it suitable as a base for supporting the next stage of operations towards the Philippines, Taiwan and the Ryukyu Islands; the deep-water harbor at Apra could accommodate the largest ships, and the two airfields would be suitable for B-29 Superfortress bombers.

The fleet from Eniwetok began arriving off Guam on the afternoon of July 20, 1944, and the transports steamed to the southern side of the island to take station off the landing beaches. The Coast Guard transports *Cor Caroli*, *Aquarius*, *Centaurus*, and *Sterope*, the 180ft buoy tender *Tupelo*, LSTs 24, 70, 71, and 207, and seven other Navy ships with partial Coast Guard crews took

Three crewmen from a Coast Guard-manned transport in the South Pacific photographed while salvaging useful material from battered Japanese landing barges on a beach in the Solomons. (AdeQHA)

US troops clamber down the side of a Coast Guard-manned attack transport into LCVPs (Landing Craft, Vehicle & Personnel) off Empress Augusta Bay, Bougainville, where 3rd Marine Division landed in November 1943. Here, as at Tarawa and other contested landings, Coast Guardsmen also served as coxswains and gunners on the landing craft. (AdeQHA)

part in the operation. In hope of drawing defenders away from the southern beaches, the Coast Guard-manned *Arthur Middleton* made a diversionary landing further to the north; several waves of her landing craft went ashore without troops and then withdrew. At the main beaches the first wave of LVTs landed at 8.30am; as at Saipan, the amtracs had to shuttle back and forth between the outer edge of the reefs and the beach. Organized Japanese resistance on Guam lasted until mid-August, and isolated Japanese diehard units prolonged the final conquest of the island for many months.

Tinian lies less than 3 miles southwest of Saipan, and due to its closeness the assault on this island would be made "from shore to shore." The task force consisted of 214 vessels, most of which were in the amphibious groups. Naval forces subjected the Japanese on the island to air and naval bombardment beginning June 11, 1944; over the following weeks they wreaked havoc on the extensive Japanese defenses, and on July 24 the landing craft moved smoothly from Saipan to Tinian. The *Cambria* and *Cavalier* arrived off the beach to land troops, the latter serving as the flagship for Commander Reserve Transport Group and Commander Transport Division Seven. That afternoon the *Cambria* moved closer to the beach to evacuate wounded from 4th Marine

Division; although the transport had to receive casualties by breeches buoy due to the unfavorable sea conditions, during the afternoon she brought aboard 293 casualties. The capture of Tinian completed the conquest of the strategic Marianas group.

The Philippines

Although 1st Marine Division faced a grinding battle on Peleliu in the Palau Islands between mid-September and late November 1944, the conquest of the Marianas and the virtual neutralization of Japanese forces on New Guinea had cleared the path for Gen MacArthur's long-desired liberation of the Philippines. Coast Guard cutters and Coast Guard-manned ships played a significant role in this massive series of operations to clear the ten major islands in an archipelago of nearly 7,000 in all. Nearly 30 Coast Guard amphibious ships landed Marine Corps and Army troops in the Philippines, beginning with the invasion of Leyte, where major air and logistical bases would then be established for attacks on the main island of Luzon and other Japanese strongpoints.

Operation *King Two* involved 738 vessels and a landing force of more than 193,000 troops; this tremendous fleet included 35 Coast Guard vessels and seven others with partial Coast Guard crews. In addition, the Coast Guard contribution included five large transports, two attack cargo vessels, ten frigates and 12 LSTs. The invasion flotilla approached Leyte Gulf in the darkness on the night of October 19, 1944, and once inside the gulf they took up their assigned stations off two landing sites. At dawn the warships began laying down an intense and deafening bombardment, and the Coast Guard transports, veterans of many campaigns, got their craft in the water in a timely fashion. The *Aquarius* put an LCVP over the side for an advanced beach party, and these four Coast Guardsmen were the first men to land on Leyte. The Southern Force went ashore on two beaches near Dulag and the Northern Force landed at two others near San Ricardo. The Japanese forces did not contest the landings as predicted; some mortar fire fell near to the Coast Guard

December 1943: photographed from a Coast Guard-manned ship, a Japanese bomb scores a near miss during the landings by 1st Marine Division at Cape Gloucester, New Britain. (AdeQHA)

April 1944: after the landings on Aitape off the north coast of New Guinea, Coast Guardsman John C. Marco, Boatswain's Mate 1st Class, directs Coast Guard landing craft bringing in supplies. (AdeQHA)

ships, but none suffered any damage. Air opposition did not develop until later, but when it did come it was in the terrifying form of *kamikazes*.

Luzon, the largest island in the Philippine group, was invaded on January 9, 1945. Coast Guard-manned ships that participated were the *Arthur Middleton*, *Aquarius*, *Cambria*, *Callaway*, *Leonard Wood*, *Cavalier*, and ten LSTs, and seven other ships had partial Coast Guard crews. The Americans had established a beachhead 15 miles wide and 4 miles deep by the end of the first day; the Coast Guard, Navy, and Merchant Marine assisted in the landing of 68,000 troops, with equipment and supplies that equaled an incredible seven tons per man. The US divisions drove toward the capital of Manila as troops and supplies arrived daily from the beaches. The Secretary-class cutter *Spencer*, now converted into an amphibious-force flagship, helped to direct landings south of the entrance to Manila Bay on January 31. Manila was eventually captured on February 6 after fierce and prolonged street fighting, but many strongpoints across Luzon still remained in Japanese hands.

G SUPPORT SERVICES, 1942–45

1: USCG DAMAGE CONTROLMAN, USCG ACADEMY

Damage Controlmen are the Coast Guard's firefighters. This is an extremely diverse rating, and a single damage controlman in the Coast Guard has the knowledge and skills of numerous civilian professional trades. Much of the Coast Guard fireman's equipment and gear differed little from those used by his civilian counterparts, including his wide-brimmed molded helmet and fire-retardant jacket.

2: MIDSHIPMAN, USCG ACADEMY

This midshipman cadet at the US Coast Guard Academy at New London, Connecticut wears basically the same uniform as his Navy counterparts at Annapolis, differenced only by the Coast Guard gold shield on his sleeves and shoulder boards and the unique cap emblem of a silver star above a vertical gold fouled anchor.

3: USCG COMMISSARY STEWARD

As in the rest of the naval establishment, in the Coast Guard the African American stewards were set apart not only by their limited opportunities for service but also by different uniforms and insignia, and by the fact that chief stewards – introduced only during the wartime enlargement of the service – were not regarded as chief petty officers. Note the "U.S.C.G." cap insignia, worn high on the crown rather than on the band.

A Roman Catholic chaplain giving mass aboard a Coast Guard vessel somewhere in the Pacific. Navy chaplains have cared for the religious needs of Coast Guard personnel since 1929, but Father Raymond F. McManus was the first Navy chaplain assigned full-time to the Coast Guard, in April 1942. (AdeQHA)

One of these was the strongly fortified island of Corregidor, and the *Spencer*'s sister veteran of the U-boat war, the CGC *Ingham*, served as flagship for this task force – the only Coast Guard vessel that participated. The *Ingham* steamed to within 3,500 yards of San Jose Beach south of Corregidor to facilitate the landings on February 16. Within three days the troops had captured most important points on the island, raising the American flag over the scene of the US garrison's capitulation in May 1942.

Iwo Jima and Okinawa

With the Philippines firmly in American hands again, the move northward towards Japan's Home Islands continued. The initial objective was Iwo Jima, an island less than 4 miles long and just over 2 miles wide honeycombed with concealed Japanese positions. Allied planners wanted this volcanic island as an emergency air base for crippled heavy bombers returning to the Marianas from missions over Japan, as well as for fighters to escort the Superfortresses throughout their round-trip missions over the Home Islands. At 2am on February 19, 1945, US Navy warships opened a bombardment using everything available in their arsenal, from the main turret guns to the antiaircraft cannons and newly developed rockets. Soon thereafter, 100 bombers attacked the island, followed by more salvoes of naval gunfire. The amphibious forces positioned themselves off seven beaches stretching some 3,500 yards along the southeast shoreline of the island; among them were the Coast Guard-manned *Bayfield* and *Callaway*, 14 LSTs, and the submarine-chaser PC-469.

With no reefs surrounding the island the landings themselves threatened little difficulty. The ships arrived off the beaches before daylight, and began debarking troops into amtracs and lowering LCMs and LCVPs for the assault. The LVTs landed the first five assault waves, but beach conditions unfortunately did not meet the hopeful expectations of the planners. The surf broke directly on the black sand, broaching the small craft and carrying them sideways up the beaches; successive waves of landing craft had difficulty making landfall and became damaged and lost, and before long the shoreline was clogged and littered with stranded craft. The Coast Guard coxswains found it necessary to back their craft into the wind and current; the beachmasters, salvage parties, and beach parties normally kept the beaches clear, but intense Japanese mortar fire prevented them fulfilling their tasks. The coxswains in the landing craft had to take all the initiative to get to the beach, unload, and back off. The wreckage eventually caused the beach to be closed to anything smaller than an LCT until tugs and other craft could clear it for later waves to disembark troops and supplies. In time, the Coast Guard succeeded in landing the Marines along with their equipment, ammunition, rations, water, bulldozers and other vehicles. (Interestingly, both the Coast Guard-manned LST-779 and the LST-758 claimed the honor of having supplied one of the flags used during the famous photographed flag-raising on Mount Suribachi.)

The major island of Okinawa in the Ryukyu group saw the Coast Guard's final important amphibious action of the war. Operation *Iceberg* followed the same successful formula developed during previous American island landings. The objectives would be bombed and shelled for nine days by carrier aircraft and warships prior to the landings. The Coast Guard had a total of 53 ships in the operation, and another six with partial Coast Guard crews. These transports, cargo vessels, amphibious force flagships, and more than 40 LSTs and LCIs formed part of the overall fleet of more than 1,400 vessels carrying more than 548,000 soldiers, sailors and Marines. The task force arrived off

Men of a Coast Guard beach party from a USCG-manned attack transport give an abandoned Japanese machine gun the "once-over" on Saipan in the Marianas. (AdeQHA)

July or August 1944: standing beside an amtrac, battle-worn US Marines advertize their gratitude to the USCG during the invasion of Guam, in which six ships and four LSTs were wholly, and seven other ships partly manned by the Coast Guard. (National Archives)

the beaches of Okinawa on Easter morning, April 1, 1945. The Japanese chose not to defend the coastline and concentrated in their inland defenses, but repeated suicide attacks by swarms of *kamikazes* presented a continuous threat to the amphibious forces and the ships lying offshore. During these attacks the Coast Guard-manned LST-884 was hit by a suicide plane that plowed through the shipfitter's shop and into the cargo of ammunition; blazing and shaken by explosions, the landing ship was abandoned, and 24 men lost their lives.

The logistic needs of the campaign developing inland were insatiable, and the coral off the beaches at Okinawa complicated the unloading of supplies. The LCVPs and LCMs had only six hours a day, around high tide, when beaching and unloading were practicable; the beachmasters unloaded as

H **US COAST GUARD INSIGNIA, 1939–45**
(1) USCG chief petty officer's cap emblem
(2) USCG officer's cap emblem
(3) USCG Reserves (Temporary) cap emblem
(4) USCG warrant officer's cap emblem
(5) USCG surfman lapel emblem
(6) US Maritime Service officer's cap emblem
(7) US Light House Service/USCG cap emblem
(8) Medal grouping: Coast Guard Good Conduct, American Defense, Atlantic Theater, Pacific Theater, World War II Victory
(9) Rating patch, petty officer 1st class, dog/ horse handler (Beach Patrol)
(10) Patch, Coast Guard air squadron VPB-6, Greenland
(11) Rating patch, petty officer 3rd class (Port Security)

1

2

3

4

5

6

7

8

9

10

11

A Coast Guard-manned LST, loaded to the gunwales with trucks, tanks, guns, and soldiers, heads toward a palm-lined beach on Leyte Island in the Philippines. Some 35 vessels of the invasion fleet were wholly manned by the USCG, and on the night of October 19/20, 1944, four Coast Guardsman of an advance beach party from the attack transport *Acquarius* were the first US servicemen to land on Leyte.

many craft as possible at high tide, stockpiled the supplies on the beach, and then moved material inland at low tide. This kept the transports at anchor for long periods of time and offered the *kamikaze* pilots, suicide boats, and torpedo craft ample time to strike at the fleet. The 82-day battle lasted from late March through June 1945. A total of 36 Allied vessels, including 15 amphibious ships and 12 destroyers, were sunk during the Okinawa campaign, and another 368 ships, including 120 amphibious craft, were damaged. The Navy's and Coast Guard's dead exceeded their wounded, with 4,907 killed and 4,874 wounded, primarily from suicide attacks.

* * *

The Coast Guard remained active with the amphibious forces until the surrender of the Japanese Empire was formally signed on September 2. Afterwards the cutters performed various operations for the occupation forces, including mine-sweeping. The Coast Guard transports finished their major work in the Pacific by transporting thousands of men home on the so-called "Magic Carpet" trips.

The China-Burma-India theater

The Coast Guard had also sent a team of beach patrol experts to China in 1944 to help train the Nationalist Chinese Army in the use of dogs and horses for patrol and counterinsurgency duty. A total of 21 enlisted Coast Guardsmen and three officers comprised the Coast Guard team, plus three veterinary officers; flown "over the Hump," they operated near Chunking, where they trained over 500 Chinese personnel.

In addition, the Coast Guard assisted the Office of Strategic Services (OSS) in the CBI, where Coast Guardsmen were engaged in the infiltration of agents into enemy territory. Many of the Coast Guardsmen were recruited for their swimming, diving, boat-handling, and signaling skills, and formed the core of OSS Maritime Unit (MU) and Operational Swimmer Group (OSG) operations. By August 1944 there were 226 men in the Maritime Unit of the OSS, over half of them from the Coast Guard. These men in fact represented the latest chapter in a long history of Coast Guard operational and intelligence activity starting with the development of signals intelligence during the "Rum War." Through their wartime support in the fields of covert counter-intelligence, espionage, and sabotage operations in the maritime environment both domestically and overseas, such Coast Guardsmen were a unique instrument for national security, and helped to lay the foundations not only for future Coast Guard operations, but also for those of organizations as yet unformed.[4]

AFTERMATH & SUMMARY

At the end of World War II most Coast Guard Reservists were released to inactive duty or discharged. The Coast Guard returned to the control of the Treasury Department on January 1, 1946. In April 1946 the Coast Guard created the Eastern, Western, and Pacific Area commands to coordinate operations that required the assets of more than one district. Pursuant to Executive Order 9083 and Reorganization Plan No. 3, on July 16 the Bureau of Marine Inspection was abolished and became a permanent part of the Coast Guard under Treasury Department control. The Coast Guard Women's Reserve was terminated in July 1947, but was re-established in August 1949.

During World War II the Coast Guard's participation in amphibious operations was perhaps the most important war-related task that the service performed. Remarkably, the United States Coast Guard fully manned 351 naval ships and craft including 77 LSTs (Landing Ships, Tank), 75 frigates, 21 cargo and attack cargo ships, and 31 transports and attack transports. In addition, the Coast Guardsmen manned 802 cutters (those over 65ft in length), 288 ships for the Army, and thousands of smaller craft including amphibious landing craft.

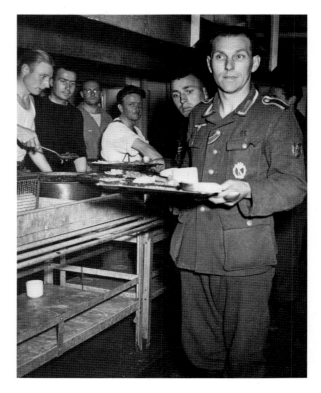

The Coast Guard-manned transport USS *Wakefield* bringing back a shipload of German prisoners-of-war for internment in America, June 1945. The expressions on the faces of some of the prisoners suggest amazement over the abundance of food and other supplies compared with war-ravaged Europe. (AdeQHA)

4 See Elite 173: *Office of Strategic Services 1942–45.*

A Coast Guard Reserve (Temporary) pipe band marching down a Boston street on VJ Day, 1945. The Temporary Reservists are wearing a combination of US Coast Guard and Scottish-style uniforms. (AdeQHA)

In all, Coast Guard crews rescued more than 1,500 survivors of torpedo attacks in waters adjacent to the United States; cutters on escort duty saved another thousand, and more than 1,500 more were rescued during the Normandy operation. Coast Guard-manned ships sank 11 enemy submarines. While on shore, armed Coast Guardsmen and Auxiliarists patrolled beaches and docks on foot, on horseback, in vehicles, with and without dogs, as a major part of the nation's anti-sabotage effort. Nearly 2,000 Coast Guardsmen died in the war, a third of those in action. Almost 2,000 Coast Guardsmen were decorated, one receiving the Medal of Honor, six the Navy Cross, and one the Distinguished Service Cross.

SELECT BIBLIOGRAPHY

Bishop, Eleanor C., *Prints in the Sand: The US Coast Guard Beach Patrol During World War II* (Missoula, MT: Pictorial Histories Publishing Company, 1989)

de Quesada, Alejandro M. "Uniforms of the Bagpipers of the United States Coast Guard and the Coast Guard Auxiliary" in *Military Collector & Historian*, Vol. 58, No. 4 (Winter 2006), pp.269–271

de Quesada, Alejandro M, *The US Home Front 1941–45*, Elite 161 (Oxford, UK: Osprey Publishing, 2008)

de Quesada, Alejandro M. "Vacationing Auxiliarists Rescue U-Boat Victims" in *Yesterday in Florida*, (No. 20, Winter 2005), p.49

de Quesada, Alejandro M. "Will what we do today be remembered tomorrow? Preserving our USCG Auxiliary History" in *Breeze*, Vol. L, No. 1 (Spring 2003), p.28. (Official publication of the USCG Auxiliary 7th Coast Guard District)

de Quesada, Alejandro M., *World War Two in Tampa Bay* (Charleston, SC: Arcadia Publishing, 1997)

"Green Uniforms Mandatory Only for Aviators, Pilots" in *All Hands,* No. 327 (June 1944), p.71

Guide for Auxiliarists Enrolled as Temporary Members of the US Coast Guard (Washington DC: US Coast Guard Auxiliary Training Unit/CGA Press, 1945)

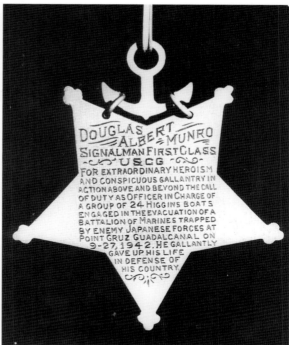

The obverse and reverse of Douglas Munro's posthumous Congressional Medal of Honor, given to his parents by President Roosevelt at the White House on May 27, 1943. The medal is currently on display at the Coast Guard Museum within the United States Coast Guard Academy at New London, Connecticut. (USCG Historian's Office)

Gummere, John F., Lieutenant, USCGR (T), *The History of The Philadelphia Regiment Volunteer Port Security Forces* (Philadelphia, PA: International Printing Company, 1946)

Pearcy, Arthur, *A History of US Coast Guard Aviation* (Annapolis, MD: Naval Institute Press, 1989)

Rankin, Col Robert H., USMC, *Uniforms of the Sea Services* (Annapolis, MD: United States Naval Institute, 1962)

Reminiscences of Your "Hitch" in the United States Coast Guard during World War II: A Pictorial Record of USCG Temporary Reserve activities in Division 5A First Naval District (Boston, MA: Division 5A Publication Committee, 1946)

Scheina, Robert L., *US Coast Guard Cutters & Craft of World War II* (Annapolis, MD: Naval Institute Press, 1982)

Skinner, Carlton, USCGR (Ret), "USS *Sea Cloud*, IX 99, Racial Integration for Naval Efficiency" (US Coast Guard Historian's Office Website: http://www.uscg.mil/History/articles/Carlton_Skinner.asp, accessed 7 September 2009)

Stacey, John A., *US Navy Rating Badges, Specialty Marks and Distinguishing Marks, 1885–1982* (pub by the author, 1982 – 11703 Old Fort Road, Fort Washington, MD 20744)

Tilley, John A., *The United States Coast Guard Auxiliary: A History 1939–1999* (Washington, DC: United States Coast Guard, 2002)

Tily, James C., *The Uniforms of the United States Navy* (New York: Thomas Yoseloff, 1964)

US Coast Guard Auxiliary: Birth to the New Normalcy? 1939–2007 (Paducah, KY: Turner Publishing Company, 2007)

Willoughby, Malcolm F., *The US Coast Guard in World War II* (Annapolis, MD: United States Naval Institute, 1957)

INDEX